# THE ANTIBIOTIC AN AILING AMERICA NEEDS

COLONEL DON WILSON

Copyright © 2020 by Colonel Don Wilson
ISBN:    Paperback    978-1-951670-26-9
         eBook        978-1-951670-28-3
         Hardback     978-1-951670-27-6

All rights reserved. No part of this publication may be reproduced, distributed, or transmitted in any form or by any electronic or mechanical means, without the prior written permission of the publisher, except in the case of brief quotations embodied in critical reviews and certain other noncommercial uses permitted by copyright law.

Ordering Information:
For orders and inquiries, please contact:
books@authorsnote360.com
www.authorsnote360.com

Printed in the United States of America

# DEDICATION

This book is dedicated to those brave heroes
who died defending this nation under God.

# CONTENTS

Introduction ................................................................. ix

Chapter 1: Who Are We? Whose Side Are We On?........ 1
               The Match That Ignited The Revolution ........ 3
               Some Just Don't Get It ................................... 8
               Lest We Forget ............................................. 11
               Obey The Commands ................................... 15
               The Ten Commandments ............................. 17
               God Hears Those Who Ask .......................... 22
               God And The Supreme Court ...................... 29
               Believer And Citizen .................................... 35
               Who Are We? Whose Side Are We On?...... 37

Chapter 2: Uncle Sam Is Annoyed! ............................... 43
               Finding Our Way Back To Eden ................. 46
               America, America! ....................................... 48
               An Outlaw Nation? ...................................... 51

Chapter 3: Balance ....................................................... 57
               The Greatest Teacher ................................... 59
               What Is Faith? .............................................. 62
               You Are Spirit .............................................. 67

Chapter 4: Living The Christian Way ........................... 70
               The Sermon On The Mount ......................... 71

Chapter 5:  A Christian World? It's Coming With
            Jesus .......................................................................89
            A Sense Of Urgency......................................... 91
            Another Way Of Saying It .............................. 92
            Church And State............................................. 99

Chapter 6:  The Two-Party System ..................... 102
            Usa Or Dsa? ..................................................... 107
            Free Will ........................................................... 109
            The End Of The Book .................................... 111

Chapter 7:  Moral Courage....................................... 115
            A Good Man .................................................... 118
            Congressional Reform ................................. 123
            Citizenship ...................................................... 126

Chapter 8:  Independence Day............................... 131

Chapter 9:  The Bill Of Rights ............................... 143

Chapter 10: Physical And Spiritual Balance = Well
            Being ................................................................. 150
            Let's Face It ..................................................... 154

Resources ............................................................................ 159

# INTRODUCTION

About eight years ago, I started a blog designed to bring traffic to my web mall. I was astounded to see it take on a life of its own. I stopped counting my reader comments at three hundred thousand. This book is a compilation of some of those blogs.

First you should understand that I speak from the perspective of an ninety-years-old who has lived an active and adventurous life as a career soldier and after retirement, a business man. I am a devout Christian and a middle-of-the-road conservative—a reflection of Winston Churchill's comment, "If you are not a liberal by the time you are twenty, you have no heart. If you are not a conservative by the time you are forty, you have no brain." As one grows in maturity, life teaches that liberalism is the Devil's playground. Yes, Satan would have us all be liberals. Liberal people and liberal government have a hard time with the Holy Bible because God commands rules for a beautiful life, without which we live a pagan existence without hope of salvation. Decline is not a condition, it's a choice; we choose to tolerate what we should stand strongly against. Therefore, we tolerate evil, error, and downright nonsense. Silence is taken as acceptance, if not agreement.

I point to a public education system that has taken God out of the classroom and thus made all sorts of bad behavior a matter of choice. Truth is no longer clear and bright but instead is blurred and obscure. If we only believed as our founding fathers did, that *truth* is that which agrees with the Word of God, we'd be far better off. Because the Bible covers every circumstance which can befall man, God's truth is the only trustworthy guide to civilization. Our all-knowing God anticipated all human folly and provides the only road to safety— His *truth*. He warns against error with all-too-human stories and provides guidance and direction. And having fallen we have the means to stand up and begin again through the love and forgiveness of our Lord and Savior Jesus Christ, who bore your sins and mine to the cross, suffering a cruel and inhuman death only to rise again after three days.

I shall authenticate my legitimate points by freely quoting the giants of our history as a nation. Our godly heritage is evident in our Constitution, many of the provisions of which were taken from the Bible by authors who were Bible educated from birth. Because the Constitution is the people's directive to the government, we became the greatest nation on earth. Because of the policies of the last two generations, we have thrown that greatness into the trash can.

It is vital that we as a people know who we are, where we came from, and where we are going. Reading this book will illuminate your rights and privileges but also your responsibilities as a citizen of this declining nation. You will learn that the assertions made here, and more to come, are true and how important it is that Americans behave themselves as God's children.

# CHAPTER 1

# WHO ARE WE? WHOSE SIDE ARE WE ON?

This is the *first* in a series highlighting America's noble heritage through the words and deeds of our founding fathers, which, with the passage of time, some of us have forgotten, and since we have forgotten, people of lesser wisdom have influenced our society in losing its way. We'll begin with some quotations reflecting the tenor of the times of our forefathers and the high priorities they held.

> The propitious smiles of Heaven can never be expected on a nation that disregards the eternal rules of order and right which Heaven itself has ordained.
> —George Washington, 1787, Inaugural Address[1]

---

[1] Unless otherwise noted, quotations taken from: William J. Federer, *America's God and Country.* (St. Louis, MO: Amerisearch, Inc. 2000).

> I therefore beg leave to move that henceforth prayers imploring the assistance of heaven, and its blessing on our deliberations, be held in this Assembly every morning.
> —Benjamin Franklin, 1787, Constitutional Convention

> I tremble for my country when I reflect that God is just; that his justice cannot sleep forever.
> —Thomas Jefferson, 1781, Notes on the State of Virginia

> It behooves us then to humble ourselves before the offended power, to confess our national sins and to pray for clemency and forgiveness...
> —Abraham Lincoln, 1863, Proclamation of National Fast

Let's go back to Benjamin Franklin, who should be a role model for all who seek elective office. He served as a diplomat, the governor of Pennsylvania, and the founder of the University of Pennsylvania and was a signer of Declaration of Independence, the Articles of Confederation, and the Constitution. He was also acclaimed as the author of *Poor*

*Richard's Almanac,* which contains many proverbs that would make King Solomon chuckle, such as, "God heals, and the doctor takes the fees." "God helps those who help themselves" (1736, not to be interpreted as stealing). "Work as if you were to live 100 years; pray as if you were to die tomorrow" (May 1757).

The careful wording of the founding documents of this nation under God shows us that God had first priority in the hearts of our founding fathers. When we as a society lose sight of that fact and fail to maintain that priority, we risk losing God's blessing and decline as a nation. Yes, in the past God has blessed our arms as we fought evil from without, but what about the evil from within that has caused the downfall of kingdoms and empires? Will America be one of these? We are headed in that direction because we have lost our way as a nation. We must regain our greatness, but not by asking, "Is God on our side?" We should be asking, "Are we on God's side?"

## THE MATCH THAT IGNITED THE REVOLUTION

This is the *second* of a series of eight articles highlighting America's noble heritage through the quotations of the most famous of our founding fathers and supporting statements of other great men and women of world history. Let us begin with a statement made by the longest-reigning monarch in history, Briton's Queen Victoria: "I so look forward to laying my crown at the feet of Jesus."

On March 23, 1775, the Second Virginia Convention had moved from the House of Burgesses to St. John's Church in Richmond because of the mounting tension between the colonies and the British king at the time. It was here that Patrick Henry's famous oration took place. We know it mostly out of context, so here is a fuller quote.

> For my own part I consider it as nothing less than a question of freedom or slavery... It is only in this way can we hope to arrive at truth, and fulfill the great responsibility which we hold to God and our country.
>
> Sir, we have done everything that could be done to avert the storm which is now coming on. We have petitioned; we have remonstrated; we have supplicated; we have prostrated ourselves before the throne, and have implored its interposition to arrest the tyrannical hands of the ministry and the parliament. Our

petitions have been slighted; our remonstrances have produced additional violence and insult; our supplications have been disregarded; and we have been spurned, with contempt. An appeal to arms and to the God of Hosts is all that is left us!

...Sir, we are not weak, if we make a proper use of the means which the God of nature has placed in our power. Three millions of people, armed in the Holy cause of Liberty, and in such a country as that which we possess, are invincible by any force which our enemy can send against us.

Besides, Sir, we shall not fight our battle alone. There is a just God who presides over the destinies of nations; and who will raise up friends to fight our battle for us. The battle, sir, is not to the strong alone; it is to the vigilant, the active, and the brave. Is life so dear, or peace so sweet, as to be purchased at the price of chains and slavery? Forbid it, Almighty God! I know not what course others may take; but as for me, give me liberty or give me death!

On June 12, 1776, Patrick Henry helped champion Article 16 of the Virginia Bill of Rights.

> That religion, or duty which we owe to our Creator, and the manner of discharging it, can be directed only by reason and conviction, not by force or violence; and therefore all men are equally entitled to the free exercise of religion, according to the dictates of conscience; and that it is the mutual duty of all to practice Christian forbearance, love, and charity towards each other.

Ordinary people confronted by extraordinary challenges and overcoming them earn the title of "Great." One of these was a graduate of the US Military Academy; a young man from America's heartland who rose to become supreme commander of the Allied Powers in Europe in WWII, president of Columbia University, and thirty-fourth president of the United States. Dwight David Eisenhower was a man of many accomplishments, most of which have been forgotten, but as we travel the interstate highway system with its convenient rest stops for our safety, we should be grateful to President Eisenhower, whose vision made it a reality. As a Republican, he presided over the greatest period of prosperity in history and yet is criticized for not doing enough by the envious big government opposition. Yes, he did nothing to limit or stifle business, our nation's biggest employer. Listen to his word as he observed the armada of three thousand ships sailing to invade Sicily in 1943:

> There comes a time when you've used your brains, your training, your technical skill, and the die is cast and the events are in the hands of God, and there you have to leave them.

In 1954 he said,

> The purpose of a devout and united people was set forth in the pages of the Bible… (1) to live in freedom (2) to work in a prosperous land…and (3) to obey the commandments of God… This Biblical story of the promised land inspired the founders of America. It continues to inspire us…
>
> The Bible is endorsed by the ages. Our civilization is built upon its words. In no other book is there such a collection of inspired wisdom, reality and hope.

## SOME JUST DON'T GET IT

Thank you for visiting my site. I will try to be a good host. This is the *third* in a series of eight articles on the subject of America's heritage told through the quotations of important figures in US and world history. Let us look at one of the most widely misunderstood subjects that by now should be clear to everybody—the true character of God. In my article entitled "Physical and Spiritual Balance," I stated that God put us here, and He expects to bring us home. Please don't disappoint Him. No matter what we've made of ourselves—sinner or saint—God loves us. He has given us a lifetime to choose where we want to spend eternity: in heaven or hell. Saints will be rewarded, and sinners will be forgiven if in this life they ask to be. God's forgiveness requires repentance, a turning away from sin, and a sincere plea for forgiveness. This act on our part enters our names in the book of life and confirms our mansion reservations in heaven. Jesus has prepared a place for you. It is waiting for occupancy. But if the judgment comes and your name is missing, to hell you go. You see, we in this short life determine our eternal destination. Remember this—you get your ticket to heaven at one exclusive agency; Jesus Christ is your Ticketmaster. There are no scalpers.

Faith gives us hope, the secret of life, and glorifying God is the purpose of life.

Faith is the acceptance of something almost without thinking, like boarding an airliner and having faith in the pilot to get us from point A to point B safely. We don't ask for his pilot license. But being human, we are constantly trying to figure things out because we can't we don't yet believe to the point of trusting God, the Creator of the universe. To illustrate, following is a quote from George Washington Carver at one of his speaking engagements:

> I always look forward to introductions as opportunities to learn something about myself…
>
> Years ago I went into my laboratory and said, Dear Mr. Creator, please tell me what the universe was made for? The Great Creator answered, "You want to know too much for that little mind of yours. Ask for something more your size little man." Then I asked, Please Mr. Creator, tell me what was man made for? Again the Creator replied, "You are still asking

too much. Cut down on the extent and improve on the intent." So then I asked, "Please Mr. Creator, will you tell me why the peanut was made?" "That's better, but even then it's infinite. What do you want to know about the peanut?" "Mr. Creator, can I make milk out of the peanut?" "What kind of milk do you want? Good Jersey milk or just plain boarding house milk?" "Good Jersey milk." Then the Great Creator taught me how to take the peanut apart and put it together again. And out of the process have come all these products.

When a story is told, there is always someone who says, "I don't get it." God's Word, the Holy Bible, tells us the truth from many different and very human points of view: Matthew, a hated tax collector who became an apostle called by Jesus; Mark, an enthusiastic young man of high principles who learned from Paul and Barnabas; Luke, a physician with the eye of a scientist for detail who learned from Peter and Phillip; and John the apostle, whose gospel is sheer poetry. In this way God made certain we'd get it, and when one of the versions come through to you, there is no trouble understanding the others.

God is good all the time. His plan for your life depends on your cooperation. We are told that God is all knowing, but there is one thing He does not know—another way to heaven than by way of His Son, Jesus.

## LEST WE FORGET

Welcome to the *fourth* in my series highlighting America's noble heritage through quotations of our founding fathers and important figures in history. I have said before, and I'll say it again, that our society has forgotten the basis, the very foundation of the American civilization. This is not new to America alone. Read these words by Rudyard Kipling, renowned British novelist, written in his noblest poem in honor of Queen Victoria's diamond jubilee in 1899.

> God of our fathers known of old—
> Lord of our far-flung battle-line—
> Dominion over pal and pine—
> Lord of hosts, be with us yet,
>
> Lest we forget—lest we forget!
>
> The tumult and the shouting dies;
> The captains and the kings depart;
> An humble and a contrite heart.

COLONEL DON WILSON

Lord of Hosts, be with us yet,
Lest we forget—lest we forget!

Far called, our navies melt away—
On dune and headland sinks the fire—
Lo, all the pomp of yesterday
Is one with Nineveh and Tyre!
Judge of the Nations, spare us yet,
Lest we forget—lest we forget!

If, drunk with sight of power, we loose
Wild tongues that have not thee in awe
Such boasting as the gentiles use
Or lesser breeds without the law—
Lord of hosts be with us yet,
Lest we forget-lest we forget!

For heathen heart that puts her trust
In reeking tube and iron shard—
All valiant dust that builds on dust
And guarding calls not Thee to guard—
For frantic boast and foolish word

Thy mercy on thy people.
Lord! Amen.

How many of us know the last two lines
of this Kipling poem penned in 1889?

East is East and West is west
And never the twain shall meet.
Till earth and sky stand presently
At God's great judgment seat.

So where is God today? Only a prayer away. Kipling said, "Oh, Adam was a gardener, and God who made him sees that half a proper gardener's work is done upon his knees."

The analogy is clear. One recent president (I'll leave you to wonder who) said, "I begin each day on bended knee."

I hope by now you see the need to place God at the top of your list of priorities. What's wrong with our ailing America? Here is at least one problem. We are not allowing God to be God, both in our government and in our daily individual lives. Also, we are moving toward socialism. Our founding fathers knew well that socialism was not the answer. History shows us it has always failed and been godless. Of course the glaring example is the Soviet Union. Its people hid their yearning for a return to the Russian Orthodox Church. While under the oppressive atheistic government, most of the faithful were like radishes—red only on the outside. If you have been following this series, you know that using faithful men, God brought our nation into being our birth as a nation.

Thomas Jefferson, third president of the United States of America, expressed the role of government well.

> A wise and *frugal* government, which shall restrain men from injuring one another, which shall leave them otherwise free to regulate their own pursuits of industry and improvement, and shall not take from the mouth of labor the bread it has earned. This is the sum of good government.

We certainly have departed from that role. A large bureaucratic government is inherently wasteful, and entrenched bureaucrats spend more time at the water cooler than at their desks. It is a monstrous drain on the taxpayers. I am reminded of the problems faced by the air force in developing a rocket capable of sending a satellite into orbit. After several aborted efforts to launch, a technician quipped, "We should name that rocket the *Civil Servant*: it won't work and you can't fire it."

History will judge men and women, no matter how prominent, by their relationship with God. Religion has done much harm to man. Saying that, you must understand that Christianity is not a religion; a religion is created by man and an outgrowth of opinion, legalistic in nature. Christianity is a personal relationship with Jesus Christ. It is the way, the truth, and the life, and no one comes to the Father except by Christ. The Christian church is not a building, but the faithful come together for mutual support and worship. Any thought or statement contradicting Holy Scripture is not Christianity.

## OBEY THE COMMANDS

Welcome to the *fifth* in my series on America's heritage. Today we are in a battle with the ACLU over, of all things, the Ten Commandments—ten rules to establish a civilized society. God gave us these rules so we might be protected from our own folly and live in a manner that will see us one day at the feet of God Himself. Our welfare, God's blessing on our nation, demands that we obey the *commands* of the Almighty. The consequences of disobedience are all around us. God has designed us so that our bodies will die one day, but our spirits are eternal; in other words, there was a time when we never were, but there will never be a time when we won't be.

We are here in this short life to make our decision: heaven or hell. Some of us don't understand this, so we are engaged in what the apostle Paul called spiritual warfare. There is an axiom in the conduct of war that says, "If you know yourself, you might win the battle, but if you know yourself and your enemy, you needn't fear the outcome of a hundred battles." Unfortunately, we have not recognized the ACLU as our enemy. These misguided people have chosen freedom as their religion and regard the Ten Commandments as an obstruction that therefore stifles freedom. God understood His creation and knew man would destroy himself unless he was obedient to rules laid down by the Supreme Being.

The case before the Supreme Court *Church of the Holy Trinity v. The United States* was summarized as follows:

> Our laws and our institutions must necessarily be based upon and embody the teachings of the Redeemer of mankind. It is impossible that it should be otherwise; and in this sense and to this extent our civilization and our institutions are emphatically Christian.

We as a people are woefully ignorant of the Ten Commandments, thus aiding the ACLU in their godless quest. This country would do well to display the Ten Commandment on billboards from coast to coast one at a time, like the old Burma Shave signs, short so the driver can read and have time to ponder them between signs. Here I will do my best to explain them so at least my readers will know them and their meaning. I think you'll find they make uncommonly good sense; after all, they are from God. God is not suggesting; He's commanding: Listen! *The italics are clarification.*

## THE TEN COMMANDMENTS

### Exodus 20

1. I am the Lord your God, who brought you out of the land of Egypt, out of a life of slavery. You shall have no other gods before Me. *Not money, not your job, not your material possessions, not your pride.*

2. You shall not make for yourself a carved image—any likeness of anything that is in heaven above, or that is in the earth beneath, or that is in the water under the earth; you shall not bow down to them nor serve them. For I, the Lord your God, am a jealous God, visiting the iniquity of the fathers upon

the children to the third and fourth generations of those who hate Me, but showing mercy to thousands of those who love Me and keep My commandments. *God is the Holy Trinity—the Father, the Son (Jesus), and the Holy Spirit, which comes to take residence in us when we are born again and transforms our very being.*

3. You shall not take the name of the Lord your God in vain, for the Lord will not hold him guiltless who takes His name in vain. *You shall not swear under oath in His name and then lie or swear or curse using His name. Jesus said, "Mention my name and I will be there." If you swear or cuss, it's like turning in a false alarm. Like the fire department, Jesus doesn't like false alarms. Bad language is not the mark of a man.*

4. Remember the Sabbath day to keep it holy. Six days you shall labor and do all your work, but the seventh day is the Sabbath of the Lord your God. In it you shall do no work: you, nor your son, nor your daughter, nor your male servant, nor your female servant, nor your cattle, nor your stranger who is within your gates, for in six days the Lord made the heavens and the earth, the sea, and all that is within them, and rested the seventh day. Therefore the Lord blessed the Sabbath day and hallowed it.

*Close up shop and turn your attention to God and family on Sunday.*

5. Honor your father and your mother, that your days may be long upon the land which the Lord your God is giving you. *This command promises long life.*

6. You shall not murder. *The Bible has many examples of God telling us to kill if our cause it is just (defense against evil) and is directed by a lawful government God established. We are not to commit premeditated murder.*

7. You shall not commit adultery. *This means having sexual relations with someone other than your spouse.*

8. You shall not steal. *This includes even the smallest thing that is not yours.*

9. You shall not bear false witness against your neighbor. *This means through actual lies or gossip.*

10. You shall not covet your neighbor's house; you shall not covet your neighbor's wife, nor his male servant, nor his female servant, nor his ox, nor his donkey, nor anything that is your neighbor's.

*Coveting can lead to adultery, theft, lies, and injury to your neighbor. Jesus said, "I give you a new commandment; love your neighbor as yourself." If you love yourself, it affects your perception of others. If you don't love yourself, you can't truly love others.*

We must do our best to obey God's law, but because of our human nature, we will fail. By observing the law, no one will be justified. The law does not save; it only condemns.

Jesus saves. If righteousness comes from observing the law, then Jesus died for nothing.

There you have it—the very foundation of the civilized world. Can you see the sense in it? There was a time when mankind lived as he pleased, the consequences of which were that man aggravated God to the point of extinction, save for one righteous man and his immediate family. Noah's faith was so strong. The fact that he lived hundreds of miles from the sea, the laughing of his neighbors, and the years it took to build the ark certainly tested his faith, but they did not deter him from carrying out God's instructions to the letter.

The atmospheric pressure and humidity at the time permitted long life (hundreds of years). Plant life was abundant and evenly distributed throughout the world, as was the wildlife. It was no trick in fill the ark with animals we think of inhabiting only certain areas of the world. After the flood, our atmosphere changed. If you think the ark story is myth, you fly in the face of plenty of archaeological proof of a worldwide flood, and as I write this, last night's news tells us a Chinese climbing party has found the ark high above the snow line of Mount Ararat (in Armenia). We'll see how this story unfolds if the media chooses to pursue it. Their recent history in such matters has been to avoid or even squelch such a story. Think of it—if our small minds can authenticate the story, it could change the world and bring salvation to millions. Sometimes politicians have intervened, deciding for themselves what's good for the public to know; upset apple carts, you know.

Faith is the assurance of things hoped for, being evidence of things not seen and the conviction of their reality (Heb. 1:11). To some it seems intangible; how can you put a price on joy and peace in your heart and mind? Stress evaporates, along with stress-related illnesses. As I write this, it occurs to me that the sooner you come to the Lord, the longer you'll live. On *The Today Show*, Willard celebrates those reaching one hundred years and older. They attribute their longevity to clean living and their faith in God. Now can you tell me what's wrong with displaying the Ten Commandments in public places? What if it does offend some sinner? Tough! The United States of America is a Christian nation. We are tolerant of other religions, yes, but remember that in a democracy the majority rules. And remember, the Bible is like a caged lion. Set him free, and he'll defend himself.

## GOD HEARS THOSE WHO ASK

Thanks for hearing me out. Your interest in what I have to say about America's godly heritage has brought you to part *six* of the series of eight, but this is not my last word on our relationship with our Savior. In any relationship, there must be communication; it is vital in a fulfilling marriage, which is God's ordinance, and in our relationship with Him, which is His purpose for our being. Our founding fathers knew that more things are wrought by prayer than this world dreams. True men of the cloth, when offering prayers in public, wax eloquent not only to request but also to touch the emotions of their audience in order to strengthen their faith.

Not long ago I invited an agnostic friend to attend a Promise Keepers rally with me. After the session, he turned to me and asked to be taught how to pray. To a Christian, there is no joy like seeing a soul saved before your own eyes. He was motivated to pray, but what held him back was the erroneous notion that prayer was complicated. All the prayers he had heard in public were eloquent, and he was not an eloquent speaker. He felt God deserved the very best prayer he could offer. I told him that prayer, like the gospels, should be simple and honest. The shortest prayer is simply, "Help me, Lord."

Before a meal, Pa Kettle looked up and uttered just two words: "Much obliged." The Bible tells us to pray in the name of Jesus. Too often people in authority create policy out of ignorance and without researching the consequences. A case in point is the Pentagon forbidding military chaplains from praying in the name of Jesus. What they don't comprehend is without the authority of Jesus' name, the prayer is just thrown up in the air and never reaches God. I wonder how many battles we'll lose before the Pentagon wakes up to their error. Political correctness is no excuse for such blasphemy. We won WWII not because God was on our side but because we were on God's side. We were instruments of God's will in stamping out the Axis evil: Mussolini, Hitler, and Tojo, in that order.

So how do we pray? Prayer is a conversation with God where we are absolutely honest and sincere in the confession of our sins, admitting our mistakes and thanking God for His forgiveness. Yes, our sincerity will bring God's forgiveness. Remember, there are no dark places in your mind, heart, and soul that God can't see into with absolute high definition. It's just not possible to fool God. You can't hide anything from the all-knowing God, so don't try. He knows your needs before you ask, but He'll do nothing about them until you ask. We must believe God has a plan for our lives; the problem comes when we interfere with His plan. Following His map will keep us on the right road. His map is called the Holy Bible, our book of instructions on how to build a joyful life. To a Christian, happiness is a series of periodic highs, and joy is a permanent way of life.

When the apostles asked Jesus to teach them to pray, He gave them what amounted to an outline to be followed, an example of the content. Christians over the centuries have committed it to memory and recite it word for word: the Lord's Prayer. The problem with reciting by rote is that it is like a machine running without thought. So let's examine the Lord's Prayer with some thought behind it. *The italics are commentary.*

> Our Father who art in heaven... *He is our Father, and we are His children. It follows that since He is the King of Kings, we are royalty in His sight—with a whole lot to learn but nevertheless princes and princesses. Even if the world*

*thinks you are a nobody, God knows you are a VIP, so hold your head up high.*

Hallowed be your name… *We must hold Him as holy and His Word the ultimate authority in all matters. We are letting God know He has first priority in our lives.*

Your Kingdom come, Your will be done on earth as it is in heaven… *The kingdom of heaven is within us when we are born again and we desire to do His will in all things. If this takes place, we'll have a pretty fair facsimile of heaven here on earth. I say facsimile because the mind of man can't possibly imagine what is in store for us in that heavenly paradise.*

Give us this day our daily bread… *Thank You, Lord, we know all we have comes from Your bounty.*

Forgive us our trespasses as we forgive those who trespass against us. *If we cannot forgive, we cannot be for-*

*given. Nursing a grudge is like a poison we take hoping the other person dies. The offender probably doesn't know he offended you, so he goes on his merry way and you are stuck with poison in your heart.*

Lead us not into temptation, but deliver us from evil… *Protect us, Lord, from the evil one by giving us the strength to resist and turn away from sin so no evil can harm us while we are under Your sheltering arms.*

For yours is the kingdom and the power and the glory forever and ever… *We close by acknowledging His preeminence in the universe.*

Can you see now how we can use the Lord's Prayer as a guide in phrasing our own prayers? First, we recognize who He is and our relationship with Him. Second, we hold Him as first priority in our life. Third, we will do our best to obey His Word so life can be beautiful. Fourth, we take stock of our blessings. Fifth, we ask His protection. Sixth, we lay our lives at the foot of the throne of the Almighty.

We must understand that God always answers prayer—maybe not in the way we'd like Him to, but always. For example, He might say no if your prayer is selfish and unworthy. Then again, He might say, "The timing of your request does not fit My plan for you just yet." Or He might say you are not mature enough to handle what you're praying for. But if your prayer is worthy, the timing is right, and you can handle it, He says, "Go for it with My blessing."

Yes, God has a plan for your life and our country. In the words of Abraham Lincoln,

> If it were not for my firm belief in an overruling Providence, it would be difficult for me, in the midst of such complications of affairs, to keep my reason on its seat. But I am confident that the Almighty has His plans, and will work them out; and, whether we see it or not, they will be the best for us.

In June of 1863, just weeks before the Battle of Gettysburg, a college president asked Lincoln if he thought the country would survive. President Lincoln replied,

> I do not doubt that our country will come through safe and undivided.

> But I do not rely on the patriotism of our people...the bravery and devotion of our boys in blue...(or) the loyalty and skill of our generals...but the God or our fathers, who raised up this country to be the refuge and asylum of the oppressed and downtrodden of all nations, will not let it perish now. I may not live to see it. I do not expect to see it, but God will bring us through safe.

One paragraph of a speech President Lincoln made on March 30, 1863 sums up my motivation for this series.

> But we have forgotten God. We have forgotten the gracious Hand which preserved us in peace, and multiplied and enriched and strengthened us; and we have vainly imagined, in the deceitfulness of our hearts, that all these blessings were produced by some superior wisdom and virtue of our own.

If you want to know if you are a Christian, ask the question: Does Jesus live through me?

## GOD AND THE SUPREME COURT

**Equal Justice under Law**

There are those who think the Bible is ancient and outdated. They reason that much of it cannot be applied to modern times. It seems that technology has become our new god. And as the ancient Greeks had many gods, and even recognized an "unknown god" in case they missed one, we worship gods of our own choice. We manufacture a god to suit our convenience. I speak of overvaluing our stuff (materialism), our jobs, money, fashion, and sex. Which of these occupy first place in your heart; which is your god? Is keeping up with the Joneses a priority in your life? Stop and think about it. What is your priority? Have you drifted away from God's will for your life, or did you even know He had a plan for your life? If so, I offer in evidence what, as a good citizen, you should know.

In my series America's heritage, we establish that almighty God guided our founding fathers in the birth of "one nation under God," but there are those among us attempting to rewrite history. Allow me to refresh their minds and point out the damage they are doing. First, let me quote the father of our country, George

Washington, who said, "Our Constitution is a miracle, surely it was written by the finger of God." Lacking a Christian education is our modern-day problem. A Christian education enables one to recognize evil in any of its forms and teaches that God is love and His Word is eternal and uninfluenced by passing fashion.

His Word is the same yesterday, today, and throughout all eternity. God's Word tells us we are not human beings on a spiritual journey; we are spirit beings on a human journey. There was a time when we never were, but there will never be a time when we won't be. We are here on this earth to overcome our evil nature—to exercise our God-given free will to choose our permanent residence for eternity: heaven or hell. Who can question Almighty God? He put us here, and He wants to bring us home, but it is our choice; we had better get it right. God said, "If my people who are called by My Name will come to me, I will heal their land." (2 Chronicles 7:14). A Christian education is the antibiotic for a sick nation.

In the United States Supreme Court in 1931, in the case of *United States v. Macintosh,* Justice George Sutherland delivered the decision regarding a Canadian seeking naturalization by reiterating the court's decision of 1892.

> We are a Christian people...according to one another the equal right of religious freedom, and acknowledge with reverence the duty of obedience to the will of God.

In the United States Supreme Court in 1948, in the case of *McCollum v. Board of Education,* Justice Felix Frankfurter delivered the court's decision.

> Traditionally, organized education in the Western world was Church education. It could hardly be otherwise when the education of children was primarily study of the Word and ways of God. Even in the Protestant countries, where there was a less close identification of Church and State, the basis of education was largely the Bible, and its chief purpose inculcation of piety...

In the United States Supreme Court in 1952, in the case of *Zorach v. Clauson,* Justice William O. Douglas delivered the court's decision, stating,

The First Amendment, however does not say that in every respect there shall be a separation of Church and State. Rather, it studiously defines the manner, the specific ways, in which there shall be no concert or union one on the other.

That is the common sense of the matter. Otherwise the state and religion would be aliens to each other—hostile, suspicious, and even unfriendly... Municipalities would not be permitted to render police or fire protection to religious groups. Policemen who helped parishioners into their place of worship would violate the Constitution. Prayers in our legislative halls; the appeals to the Almighty in messages of the Chief Executive; the proclamation making Thanksgiving Day a holiday; "so help me God" in our courtroom oaths—these and all other references to the Almighty that run through our laws, our public rituals, our ceremonies, would be flouting the First Amendment. A fastidious atheist or agnostic could even object to the supplication with which the Court opens each session: God save the United States and this Honorable Court.

We are a religious people and our institutions presuppose a Supreme Being. When the state encourages religious instruction or cooperates with religious authorities by adjusting the schedule of public events to sectarian needs, it follows the best of our traditions.

For it then respects the religious nature of our people and accommodates the public service to their spiritual needs. To hold that it may not would be to find in the Constitution a requirement that the government show a callous indifference to religious groups. That would be preferring those who believe in no religion over those who do believe…

> We find no constitutional requirement makes it necessary for government to be hostile to religion and to throw its weight against the efforts to widen the scope of religious influence. The government must remain neutral when it comes to competition between sects…

> We cannot read into the Bill of Rights such a philosophy of hostility to religion.

Now there are a lot of people that will read this and say, "Yes, but." and litigate nitpicking points, even going as far as to the Supreme Court, which has picked apart these nits ad infinitum. To go deeper into this subject, I highly recommend the source I've been using: the book titled *America's God and Country*.[2] It is an encyclopedia of quotations by William J. Federer. It is a great resource for use in speeches, papers, debates, and essays.

Lawyers sometimes win cases based on precedence—that is, if a lawyer can show a judge similar cases where the outcome was what the lawyer is after, he strengthens his case. In my mind, each case must be decided on its own merits. I am reminded of Winston Churchill's quip, "Precedence embalms principle." By the way, he also said, "If by the time you are twenty you are not a liberal you have no heart, and if by forty you are not a conservative you have no brain." Yes, over time we mature and gain, with experience, practical knowledge. At ninety I have learned that a conservative outlook on life makes it so much easier to walk with God.

---

[2] Ibid.

## BELIEVER AND CITIZEN

Let me draw the parallel for you. Our country has never been perfect, nor will it ever be, but it has been head and shoulders above the rest. Our founding fathers did their very best to conceive a government of the people, by the people, and for the people. They could not have designed a system of government as functional and protective of the people without divine guidance. It just could not have happened unless God was in it. As the years have passed, we have grown and maintained our sovereignty by protecting our Constitution.

We have become the most powerful nation in the world by minding our own business until threatened by others or when help was requested by our allies. Only then have we intervened, pulling their chestnuts out of the fire, thereby keeping war away from our shores. In doing so, we have not acquired one inch of conquered ground. In fact, we poured many dollars into rebuilding Germany and Japan after WWII. I love my country. I gave my youth in its service joining the army at eighteen and retiring at forty-one. I am a veteran of the Korean War and served in Vietnam. At ninety I still love my country, but I hate to see what the last two generations have done to it.

The Christian, no matter how devout, is not perfect; we are a work in progress. And so it is with our nation.

Unfortunately, like a large percentage of professing Christians, our nation has distanced itself from church and has backslidden at an alarming rate. We have forgotten God and in doing so forgotten our heritage. Leaving God out of our private lives only condemns the individual to unnecessary despair, error, and suffering, without realizing it has done a disservice to our country. As Alexis de Tocqueville predicted, "As long as America is good she will be great. When she ceases to be good she will cease to be great." Our beloved country no longer occupies the lofty position it once held among nations and has lost God's blessing in the process. This may sound a little strange to you, but listen. The church, as Jesus chose to call it, is of God, by God, and for God, and no matter what the secular world may do or say, it shall not perish from the earth. It never has, and it never will. God loves us and wants to protect us from our own folly. He has provided the Holy Scriptures for our education.

We as individual citizens, while proceeding with our Christian education, must also study simple civics to understand the built-in checks and balances that prevent any one branch of our government from seizing absolute power. We the people must hold their feet to the fire in order to make each branch properly execute their *constitutional* prerogatives (i.e., Congress should not let the Supreme Court legislate from the bench). I know it is very tempting for a career politician to avoid a controversial vote that could lose votes in the next election and to pass the buck to the court. This is another reason for *term limits.* Citizen legislators serving one or two terms will do what's right for the country without fear of losing their jobs.

## WHO ARE WE? WHOSE SIDE ARE WE ON?

Inevitably, entrenched career politicians will resist giving up their power by giving more "free" handouts to their constituents. That's when the death march toward socialism is well underway. Ronald Reagan put it this way, "How do you tell a communist? Well, it's someone who reads Marx and Lenin. How do you tell an anti-communist? It's someone who understands Marx and Lenin."

I often wonder if the average American has any idea of how our government is structured or functions. Take a look. Our founding fathers designed a system to curb the abuse of power. The *Constitution is the people's directive to the government* and therefore must not be violated. Just so, the *Holy Bible is God's directive to the people,* by which we must live.

| Constitution | | |
|---|---|---|
| Legislative Branch | Executive Branch | Judicial Branch |
| Senate | President | Supreme Court |
| House | Vice President | |

First and foremost, all our elected and appointed officials are by oath pledged to support and defend the Constitution of the United States of America. The legislative branch can pass a bill, but if the president determines it to be a bad bill, he can refuse to sign it, thus vetoing the bill. If congress feels the president is exceeding his powers, they can override the veto by a two-thirds vote. Then, of course, the Supreme Court can declare the bill or any action by the congress or the president unconstitutional without fear of losing their jobs because they are appointed for life. There are nine Supreme Court justices, so there can be no tie vote.

Our Constitution gives each branch a means to prevent the seizure of absolute power. But if a president, who appoints Supreme Court justices, is in power too long, he has the chance to load the court with his own henchmen as justices die or retire or are persuaded to retire. The government is in place to do the bidding of the people. Our Constitution guarantees this, and if functioning properly, that guarantee is enforceable. But we have another problem that obstructs the founding fathers' intent: the career politician.

**The Evils of Power**

It was intended that we have a citizen-represented government of the people, by the people, and for the people with majority rule. The old saying "Absolute power corrupts absolutely" is evidenced by today's events. Corruption in the business world and government is front-page stuff these days. I present the following quotes of our founding fathers regarding the original intent of our government.

John Adams, second president of the United States (on elections) said, "Elections to office which are great objects of ambition, I look at with terror."

James Madison, fourth president of the United States, said,

> Whenever there is an interest and power to do wrong, wrong will gen-

erally be done and not less readily by a powerful and interested Party, than a prince... "Wherever the real power in a government lies, there is a danger of oppression. In our government, the power lies in the majority of the Community...government is the mere instrument of the major number of constituents.

Thomas Jefferson, third president of the United States, said,

> The whole art of government consists in the art of being honest... The will of the public majority should prevail. ...The general (federal) government will tend to monarchy, which will fortify itself from day to day, instead of working its own cures. ...What country can preserve its liberties if their rulers are not warned from time to time... It is the manners and spirit of the people which preserves a republic in vigor. A degeneracy in these is a canker which soon eats the heart of its laws and constitution.

## THE ANTIBIOTIC AN AILING AMERICA NEEDS

> A group of U.S. Senators recently introduced a constitutional amendment that would apply *term limits* to all members of Congress... Arguing that the only way to change the policies coming out of Washington is to change the process, DeMint and others have proposed a most radical step, one that strikes directly at the heart of the power structure inside the national capital, but one that is consistent with the voter outrage directed at the big spending, grow the government initiatives coming out of the White House and the Reid-Pelosi Congress...
> —*US News and World Report*[3]

Americans know real change in Washington will never happen until we end the era of permanent politicians. When a government can ram policies down our throats against the will of the majority, that's called tyranny, and that means the voters have lost their franchise, and that means oppression, and that means the people have lost their power, and that means socialism, which

---

[3] US News and World Report quote taken from mailed request to support term limits. Senator DeMint

has always failed wherever it has been tried. Don't we learn anything from history? Our national sovereignty and our very freedom are in serious jeopardy. Wake up, America, before it's too late. Kick the career politicians out by listening to our founding fathers and setting *term limits* so "that government of the people, by the people and for the people shall not perish from the earth."

## CHAPTER 2

# UNCLE SAM IS ANNOYED!

He's telling the ACLU to take a history lesson!

Prior to, during, and after WWII, there were many subversive organizations that were monitored by the FBI hiding behind high-sounding titles that masked their real agenda. I am reminded of these when I consider the ACLU. If liberty is to be used in their title, they should at least know the meaning of the word. Freedom without responsibility is anarchy. Do you recall the four freedoms?

- Freedom of speech
- Freedom of worship
- Freedom from want
- Freedom from fear

> Men must be led by God or they'll be ruled by tyrants.
> —William Penn

We live in a land that welcomes people seeking liberty, citizenship, and freedom from religious persecution. We must not cheapen the rights of citizenship by offering its privileges to illegal aliens. Citizenship must come first, and then come the benefits. In this way we will maintain our strength and unity as a sovereign nation. We are also an English-speaking nation. A common language is an important component of our unity. Regardless of how broken, a citizen must speak English.

A case that went before the Supreme Court, *Church of the Holy Trinity v. US,* is summarized thus:

> Our laws and our institutions must necessarily be based upon and embody the teachings of the Redeemer of mankind. It is impossible that it should be otherwise; and in this sense and to this extent our civilization and our institutions are emphatically Christian.

It is a fact that above the head of the chief justice of the Supreme Court the Ten Commandments are carved in stone with the great American eagle protecting them. At the beginning of each session of the court, as the justices stand before their desks, the crier opens with the invocation: "God save the United States and this Honorable Court."

What does the inscription on the Statue of Liberty say?

> Give me your tired, your poor, your huddled masses yearning to breathe free; the wretched refuse of your teeming shore. Send your homeless, tempest tossed to me. I lift my lamp beside the golden door.

Remember, Uncle Sam is the symbol of majority rule. The tail does not wag the dog!

And finally, here is one last word from a true statesman:

> Christianity is the companion of liberty in all its conflicts—the cradle of its infancy, and the divine source of its claims."
> —Alexis de Tocqueville, 1840
> (French statesman and historian)

Our precious citizenship should not be a watered-down version of our founding fathers' vision. Their vision has been paid for with the shed blood of many generations. Let not their sacrifice be in vain.

## FINDING OUR WAY BACK TO EDEN

There is absolutely no one on this earth, be he pope or bum, president or dog catcher, who doesn't need God's forgiveness. Adam and Eve had it made; they were without sin and companions to God until they disobeyed God's specific instructions not to eat or even touch the fruit of the tree of the knowledge of good and evil (Genesis 3:30). They were cast out of the garden of Eden, where all was provided for them, and placed in a comparably desolate land to scratch the earth for survival. From that day on, mankind needed God's forgiveness because they were no longer sinless but instead were born with a sinful nature. Adam's first son murdered his brother. To gain God's pardon, we have to be born again; that is to say, we must be reborn in spirit to worship God through His Son Jesus, the Christ; the translation from the Greek is the anointed one.

In the simplest of terms, at the moment we accept Jesus into our minds and hearts, we become citizens of heaven, as welcome as Jesus Himself; the Bible calls us co-heirs of the kingdom. Imagine that no matter how black your past, you have become as white as snow and

God forgets your past sin, no matter how heinous. From here on, it's up to you; you are born again, with a clean slate. How many of us wish we could start over because of the mistakes we have made? Well, here's your only chance. It's your choice; you can live with your mistakes or start fresh with the Holy Spirit to guide you.

It has always been a joy to see the transformation in a person who has taken Jesus to heart and joined with fellow believers in the study and worship of God. They are lifted up out of themselves. Minor and serious problems and addictions seem to melt away as they learn to view life from a Christian perspective. The love of God and their neighbor has made new people out of them; their language is cleaned up, and their anger is toned down; anger becomes righteous indignation. What's more, they come to realize that words can not only inspire, but they can also hurt; they can now understand why God calls gossip a sin.

I just said they become new people; what I mean is they become better, more loving people, making friends more quickly and becoming eager to serve and in doing so, earning the respect of people who, observing their new lifestyle and its advantages, want to know more about this man Jesus who lives in them.

No day should pass without some stranger coming to realize that you are a practicing Christian by your words or actions. There are many opportunities in a day to convey that fact; how about answering "Have a nice day," with "And God bless your day too." You'll be surprised at how many thanks you get, along with a smile of recognition from Christian brothers or sisters who are not permitted references to God by those in management, who are dictated to by that nasty and compromising phrase, "political correctness."

Political correctness is another term for evading the issue, the issue being the truth. What we tolerate, we teach. How can a Christian nation tolerate atheism, pornography, homosexuality, abortion, and prohibitions against teaching values tied to the authority of Christ? All of the above were the seeds of the destruction of empires from within.

The warning signs are clear, America—straighten up and fly right; or better said, look to God and soar in righteousness. Yes, children, behave yourselves!

## AMERICA, AMERICA!

What have you become? Oh, what would you be today if you had practiced the presence of God? Today we are learning the cost of being the culture of the comfortable. The Bible warns that when we take pride in our prosperity—thinking what a great job we've done without the help of God—that is when we are weakest and most vulnerable to Satan's attacks. Jesus asked, *"How has the city on the hill become a harlot? Everything was going well, and now it has become a city of murder and hate."* (Isaiah 1:21). Hello, America!

To the world, America has been the bright city on the hill, an example of liberty, religious freedom, and free enterprise. But today it is a country that has little regard for history. We don't remember the real reasons for the Great Depression. The immorality and greed of the 1920s were the excesses that caused a twelve-year depression, with the unemployed standing in line for their daily bread and soup doled out by government and charities. Veterans marched on Washington, DC, asking for the government-promised bonus they never received. In an attempt to create jobs, the government formed the Civilian Conservation Corps (CCC), a quasi-military organization that, among other chores, developed our National Parks infrastructure, and the Works Progress Administration (WPA), a public works organization. These required an act of congress called the National Recovery Act (a.k.a., the NRA). All this alphabet soup got some needed work done, but it took a second world war to put everyone back to work and war bonds to help finance it.

Knowing this, how could we let it happen again? We haven't been exposed to the lessons of history. The dead past was not made alive again by competent education that included the influence of God on our history.

Yes, bemoan our economy all you wish, but you must admit that we brought its troubles upon ourselves. There is an old adage: "History repeats itself." There is also another: "Your thoughts manage your life." You must keep your thoughts on God's truth and the positive. You must know who you are, where you came from, and how you got here. With the advancement of science, we now know the Bible to be more than theology; it is the history book of its time. You only need to read Isaiah, written hundreds of years before Christ (BC) to find accurate prophesies that came true in the life of Jesus. Everything from the Christmas story to the crucifixion is predicted in amazing detail, and the evidence is irrefutable.

Without God's truth we poison the thoughts of our children and sentence them to a sick life. Here is a true example. Without corroboration or support from the secular world, and with some contradiction by the school's teaching, a son dismissed his mother's godly teaching. He led a reckless, dope-addicted life and was constantly on the police blotter for some crime or other. Finally, in a desperate mood, he attended church with his mother. This was ten years ago. Recently, we added a new young pastor to our staff and assigned him the duties of youth pastor. Our retired senior pastor thought he recognized the young man and approached him, asking, "I know you, don't I?" The young pastor said, "Yes, you know me. I'm Ethel's boy." Imagine going from delinquent to pastor. That's redemption; that's beginning again. Some who knew the young man called it a miracle.

It can all happen when you practice the presence of God.

Let me add this thought: Remember, only two defining forces have ever offered to die for you—Jesus Christ and the American soldier. One died for your soul, the other for your freedom.

## AN OUTLAW NATION?

So you say you are a good person, a law-abiding citizen? I've got news for you: we are a nation of outlaws. I'd be safe in saying we as individuals violate the law at the very least once a day. When was the last time you broke the speed limit? How about that parking ticket or taking office supplies home from work? Oh, there must be thousands of ways we break the law, but let's narrow it down to ten—God's law, from which our civilization was built. Yes, I've made my point, but let's narrow our violations down to one that undermines the very foundation of civilization. When was the last time you attended church? If you answered that question with "Never," "Hardly ever," "Easter Sunday," "Christmas," or "Once in a while," you have broken God's law, specifically the fourth commandment. Here is what is says:

> Six days you shall labor and do all your work, but the seventh day is the Sabbath of the Lord your God. *In it* you shall do no work: you, nor your son, nor your daughter, nor your wife, nor your male servant, nor your female servant, nor your cattle, nor your stranger who is within your gates.
>
> For in six days the Lord made the heaven and the earth, the seas, and all that is in them, and rested the seventh day. Therefore, the Lord blessed the Sabbath day and hallowed it. (Exodus 20:11).

The Sabbath is to be a holy day, set aside to God. The Hebrew word means to "rest." (Webster's New World Dictionary). One who is in a covenantal position with God is to stop the everyday activities of life and honor God with rest every seventh day. God set the pattern in creation: for six days He worked; on the seventh day, He rested.

It is not what we do to gain God's pleasure but not doing what God wants us to do that displeases Him. God demands one day in seven to be holy and devoted to Him in order to refresh our faith and renew the body and soul for the week to come. On one day in seven we are to turn to God and humble ourselves. This not only pleases God, but by carrying His Word with us through the next six days, we please Him even more.

So you see, if we violate the law, we are no better than the wicked, and God told us,"*There is no peace for the wicked.*" (Isaiah 57:21). All businesses (except emergency services) that remain open on the Sabbath are violating God's law. I was stationed at Fort Hood, Texas, in 1960. The local civilian communities had what was called a blue law, which took God at His word and closed businesses on Sunday. Woe to the door-to-door salesman who tried to work on the Sabbath. He had no chance of making a sale on Sunday. More often than not, doors were slammed in his face.

We tend to think some crimes are more serious than others. We give them labels: capital crimes, felonies, misdemeanors, or petty crimes. However, God's law (singular) includes ten parts; break just one part and you break the whole law, in God's sight. That goes for the new commandments taught by Jesus, who was God with us and continues to live in the hearts of Christians everywhere. So we are all outlaws. We need regular church attendance to humble ourselves before God and ask His forgiveness. Your sins are not forgiven until you ask in prayer because God wants to hear from you frequently. There is nothing difficult about prayer; you simply talk to God as a child to his or her father, for advice or forgiveness. This is an act of faith that pleases God.

Matthew 12:11-12 clarifies work of the Sabbath.

> What man is there among you who has one sheep, and it falls into a pit on the Sabbath, will not lay hold of it and lift it out? Of how much more value than is a man than a sheep? Therefore, it is lawful to do good on the Sabbath.

Mark 2:27-28 says, "The Sabbath is made for man, and not man for the Sabbath. Therefore the Son of Man is also Lord of the Sabbath."

A few years ago, Christian producers traveled to the churches of this country with a play. They enlisted local talent found in the churches to present the play. It was about people of various circumstances facing the judgment of God. One episode depicted a mother who was too busy to attend church herself, but she dropped her little daughter at church each Sunday morning. The little girl was embraced by Jesus, but the mother was whisked away by Satan with his diabolical laugh. The mother thought she was doing good, but she had no time for a personal relationship with God.

We must also demonstrate our faith as a nation of righteous people living as one nation under God. It is unfortunate that the character and integrity of the people have been downgraded by the generation of "enlightenment"—producing leaders who are immoral and dishonest, ready to compromise their integrity. We call them professional politicians.

We are not all fooled by the professional politicians. Recently I heard this: Recall the recent earthquake on the East Coast that damaged the Washington

Monument. Some say it was caused by our founding fathers turning over in their graves. Others say it was a federal check bouncing. Seismologists discovered a new fault in Virginia that extends beneath the District of Columbia. They are calling it Obama's Fault.

God's law is to be obeyed; look what disobedience has cost us. We must not continue as outlaws or allow ourselves to be led by outlaws. We must hold our teachers and leaders to a higher standard than other professions; God does.

## CHAPTER 3

# BALANCE

We have been taught that justice is blind. The scales of justice can represent *good and evil, guilt and innocence, or justice and injustice,* but did you know that God has a balance scale for life? His scale tells us that He is a jealous God because it represents *prosperity and adversity*

He is watching the scale of your life closely for balance. What do I mean by balance? It means that in this life, you must have equal shares of prosperity and adversity. Why? Remember, He is a jealous God. Too much prosperity leads to greed and self-satisfaction. You may think you did in all by yourself without God's help. Adversity causes you to ask God for help. When you are too prosperous and have an inflated opinion of yourself and your abilities, ignoring God, He will drop some adversity on the scale to balance your life. The weight of this adversity depends on how far you've drifted from God's Word. It can be disastrous, like the collapse of your business, fines, and prison terms. We have seen the results of corruption in American life, and it has cost us as individual investors and as a nation.

Most politicians, professors, teachers, managers of businesses, parents, and children of this generation were taught in ungodly education programs, which set us up for corruption, immorality, and in general, bad behavior in violation of the Ten Commandments. Justice would say we have been naughty and are in need of punishment. Adultery is common in today's society, from the president to young marrieds. Fornication is common to all ages, and we call it recreational sex. But God is ready to forgive all if we will ask it and return to Him.

What does God want from us? He gave us the Word; teach it! A Christian education is the antibiotic an ailing America needs. We can teach the Bible without evangelism. Teachers need not try to convince; God's Word does that. The student is still capable of making a choice. That choice is what life is all about and why we are here—to give spiritual balance to our lives and behave ourselves. As we have seen, the consequences of our misdeeds are far worse than standing in the corner.

## THE GREATEST TEACHER

Almighty God made us. He knows us so well that He sees right through us. We cannot hide our deepest, darkest thoughts from Him. He knows what you need before you ask. You may be asking for something that will hurt you or something you can't handle. God knows what is best for you and will answer your prayers accordingly. Basically, God will answer your prayer in one of three ways: no, not yet, or okay. He has good reasons for each answer, and they are all for your benefit. God is in control, not you, even though you might think you are. To live a great life, you must follow the advice of your Father—your heavenly Father—and adhere to His teachings because they are ultimate truth. Be honest; you don't want to live a lie, do you?

This is as close to writing an essay as I care to get. This is a blog to point the way to God's content, the book of life, and instructions for victorious living by the Creator of life itself. What greater credentials could you ask?

Here I'm going to list some of the lessons He wants to teach you—lessons using flawed people just like you and me (some worse and some better, but none perfect) to make His points in a powerful and memorable way.

- Don't underestimate the importance of reading and understanding God's Word.
- At times you may become the answer to your own prayers.
- Your life should be seen and measured in light of eternity.
- Nothing in this life will bring true meaning and happiness—not wealth, fame, pleasure, or success. Only trust in God can lead you to real fulfillment.
- There is much less that you can depend on than you think!
- True happiness comes only from obedience to God.
- Faith is not a one-time act. It's a way of life.
- You are called to trust God—even when life seems impossible and incomprehensible.
- The wicked may appear to be victorious, but ultimately our righteous God will punish them.
- God's ways are not our ways. They are beyond our understanding.
- Jesus is God among us. He shows you the Word of God is your best defense against the enemy of your soul.
- Jesus has conquered the power of death and provides the only path to overcoming it.

- Jesus has entrusted His message to His disciples, or His followers. You become a follower when you trust in Him.
- Jesus did not merely preach abstract religious ideas but a new way of living.
- You are commanded not to worry but rather to give all your concerns to God and allow Him to take care of them.
- Even your most difficult circumstances can have positive benefits and be cause for rejoicing.
- Your conduct should point unbelievers to Christ, especially those in your family.
- You should not be surprised when persecution comes.
- Jesus is coming again!

It would use all the space on this computer to list all the lessons our great God teaches. That's why believers spend time each day learning His ways until they will go to join Him when He raptures the church. Believe me when I say God knows your name, and He knows who to take and who to leave behind. In fact, the Bible tells us that on arrival God will give me a new name for a new life for eternity. Something tells me I won't miss Donald Wilson a bit.

People who say there are other ways to go to heaven simply don't know the truth. They are only relating a "wish list," created by man, which will not be honored by God because He did not teach it. The Bible is the inerrant Word of God, and His resurrection is the basis for our faith and our civilization, which gives us the commands of God, not some small human's feeble hopes.

The Great Teacher wants to talk to you; study your Bible to hear His voice.

## WHAT IS FAITH?

When asked I asked this, my friend replied, "I don't have faith in anything."

I said, "Sure you do."

He said, "No I don't." Well, I'll tell you what I told him.

First, what is faith? It is the substance of things hoped for and the evidence of things not seen. Let me illustrate. A man is grabbing breakfast while arguing with his wife, telling his kids to shut up, and thinking, "When I come home, I'll ask for a divorce." On the way out of the house, he kicks the family dog and then jumps into the car and lays rubber leaving the driveway. While driving to work, he encounters three idiots and two morons. He arrives at the airport and reports in, files his flight plan, and heads for his 747, muttering under his breath. As it turns out, he is the pilot of your airliner. Now, not knowing any of the above, you settle into seat 12F with complete faith that the pilot will get you safely to your destination.

A woman who didn't know anything about the inner workings of an automobile has faith that the second she turns the key, the complicated machine will come to life and away she will go. Now she's on a two-lane roadway with a forty mph speed limit and has faith that the car barreling toward her will miss her by four feet. When she passes an eighteen-wheeler and cuts in front of him too closely, she has faith that his brakes are good enough to stop short if need be. By some miracle, she arrives home in one piece and has faith that when she presses the button on her remote, the garage door will open and another remote will turn on the TV. She flips the bathroom switch, having faith the light will go on, and then she turns on the bath water, having faith it will be hot. I think I've made my point. Each day we exercise our faith.

The Bible says if you have faith the size of a mustard seed, you can say to that mountain, "Move!" and the mountain will move. What is your mountain? In 1963 I was thirtythree and had a two-pack-a-day habit. Smoking was my mountain. I had read the surgeon general's report and I wanted to quit, but how was I to break the grip of nicotine? Then one evening I was thumbing through my wife's copy of *The Ladies Home Journal* and found an article that seemed to answer my question. It told of a group of folks from all walks of life who met on Tuesday nights just to discuss smoking. Everyone had their story—some very familiar to me. But what stopped me in my tracks was a statement by a doctor in attendance. He said that after three days without a cigarette, the body gives up its demand for nicotine. It's no longer a physiological problem; it has now become a mental habit, and I must replace a habit with a habit.

Daily circumstances trigger the desire to light up: when you awaken in the morning, after that first cup of coffee, when faced with a problem, turning on the TV, after making love, seeing someone else light up or at a cocktail party. Whatever your trigger, hold off the impulse by doing something else with your hands and mind. It works because it is now a mental process, and no one wants to think of themselves as weak willed. You see, I put my faith in the doctor's statement and moved my mountain.

Jesus told us to have the faith of a little child. The thought reminds me of a mother who, during a thunder storm, was afraid for her little child. With lightning flashing, she just knew her little girl was terrified, so she dashed into her room and found her standing at the window. The child turned to her mother and said excitedly, "Mommy, God just took my picture!"

My faith was made complete by my recent tour of Israel. It went like this: at each biblical site we visited, our pastor read the Bible passage pertaining to that site, and an archeologist who turned into a pastor due to his discoveries explained the evidence of the site. When we arrived at Caesarea on the Mediterranean, we found displayed a large marble slate uncovered by archeologists. It read in deeply carved Latin that it was the summer home of Pontius Pilate (who ordered the crucifixion of Jesus). This was a nine-day tour, which I heartily recommend. It will change your life. The security of the tours is well conceived though not obvious. It is perfectly safe, and accommodations are first class. Our faith in the security was not misplaced. The fitting climax of the tour was my baptism in the Jordan River.

On the other hand, I have no faith in the big bang theory of creation. The odds are just too long. It's like an explosion in a junkyard and all the fragments falling to earth in the form of a flyable Boeing 747. No, there is a divine intelligence behind the creation of the universe. When you believe Genesis 1:1, you'll have no trouble believing the rest of the Bible. When Darwin dreamed up his theory of evolution, scientists of the time grabbed onto it like a bulldog and still cling to the outdated theory; yes, it's still an unproven theory, not fact. Even Darwin himself retracted the theory late in his life.

Science has wasted a lot of time and money searching in vain for the missing link, even going so far as to manufacture bogus evidence. They have only succeeded in making monkeys of themselves. Many have tried to refute God's Word, only to become believers after careful research. With modern technology, more and more archeological evidence has confirmed Holy Scripture. We now regard the Bible as the authentic history of the period.

Faith comes by hearing and hearing by the Word of God. Webster says faith is complete trust and reliance in God.[4] Some believe in mystics, astrologers, clairvoyants, and even Devil worship, so why is it so hard to have faith in almighty God, Creator of the universe, especially when His Word makes so much sense in the chaotic world of small-minded people? The highest IQ

---

[4] *Webster's New World Dictionary,* Fourth Edition, s.v. "faith."

in the world is but a grain of sand on the ocean shore compared to God's omniscience. I ask you to imagine—although I know you can't—God, who is the Alpha and Omega, the beginning and the end. He sees all of history and all things to come at a moment in time. He is all knowing, all powerful, and ever present. He dwells in the supernatural whereas we live in the natural. Knowing that, like my friend, we have taken the step of faith and invited the Holy Spirit, the Helper Jesus promised, into our hearts, minds, and souls. Our slates are clean. We are forgiven of our sins, past, present, and future. Does that mean we can go on sinning? Of course not! But we will sin less and less in our quest for perfection. God knows we won't achieve perfection in this world, but we must enjoy trying. Once you know your Bible, it becomes a magnificent obsession.

## YOU ARE SPIRIT

Just as God gave us four gospels through Matthew, Mark, Luke, and John to be sure we got His message, I will keep telling you what you must know and accept in your heart. To many people the Bible is a book of dos and don'ts. Do obey God's teachings. Do accept God's grace. Don't violate the Ten Commandments, etc. They don't see the love and personal protection behind God's Word.

Life as we know it and death are not divided in the spiritual sense. In our earthly life we reside in a physical body—a home for our spirits. When that body shuts down, wears out, and dies, our spirits leave our bodies at the moment of death and acquire heavenly bodies that will never suffer pain or illness and begin life in eternity. We are still alive but in a different dimension; here I speak of devout Christians. Those who in this life chose *not* to accept Jesus Christ *will* suffer pain and torment in hell. You see, they must accept responsibility for their wrong decisions.

I've told you before that there was a time when you never were, but there will never be a time when you won't be. Once God created your spirit, you live for eternity. Whether you live in heaven or hell is the crucial decision of your lifetime. No one will make that decision for you. It's up to me and other Christians to point the way; but if you won't listen, tough. You'll find hell very tough.

Now what does that decision involve? The Bible makes it plain. It is all about accepting Christ as your personal Savior and becoming the person God wants you to be. Change? Yes, but the Word will help your spirit become holy. You have been given an unbelievable gift. "God so loved the world that He gave His only begotten son that whosoever believes in Him shall not perish but have everlasting life" (John 3:16). He sent a teacher to show us the way, His Son to be God among us, who led a perfect life as an example. But—and here's the fly in the ointment—since Adam's sin, his offspring have an evil nature and fall short of the glory of God. God devised a plan to forgive us all of our sins. Jesus, who suffered pain like the rest of us, sacrificed Himself and took the burden of our sins upon Himself to the cross, giving up His life in a violent and suffering way for His friends.

Now here's the wonder of it. Not only are you forgiven your past sins but your present and future sins as well. That is why we call it the perfect gift. But here is the price: you must believe and take to your heart what Jesus told you: *"I am the way, the truth, and the life. No one comes to the Father except by me."* (John 14:5).

Believe this: hell is real. You don't want to go there. Add to the dirtiest place in a ghetto violent gangs, constant fire, pain, and depression, and you'll still have only a vague idea of just how real a place it is.

Please, friends, believe that Jesus is Lord and you will be saved. There is an afterlife; you are here to prepare for it. Do you doubt it? Go to your Bible or go to hell.

## CHAPTER 4

# LIVING THE CHRISTIAN WAY

In the Old Testament, God commanded certain behavior, and that's good. However, some humans harbor attitudes that resent absolutes (i.e. the Ten Commandments). The fact is, when we abandon absolutes, we can no longer discern between good and evil, so God gave us absolutes by command. Eventually, the elders of Israel began to lend their own erroneous interpretation to the commandments, which in God's sight was what we call legalism. This set up a situation requiring a different approach. So Jesus left the comfort of heaven and came to earth as "God among us" to set the record straight. His teaching was versed in love. He offered a reward for good behavior; He said we would be blessed. No summary of the New Testament would be complete without the Sermon on the Mount. Jesus teaches the rules for a civilized world. Listen and heed.

## THE SERMON ON THE MOUNT

**The Beatitudes**

Matthew 5

> And seeing the multitudes, He went up on a mountain, and when He was seated His disciples came to Him. Then He opened His mouth and taught them, saying:
>
> Blessed are the poor in spirit, for theirs is the kingdom of heaven. [*The poor in spirit are those who recognize their spiritual poverty and casting aside all self-dependence, seek God's grace.*]
>
> Blessed are those who mourn, for they shall be comforted. [*Those who mourn are not necessarily people in bereavement but those who experience the sorrow of repentance.*]

Blessed are the meek, for they shall inherit the earth. *[Meek does not connote weakness but rather controlled strength. The word carries the ideas of humility and self-discipline.]*

Blessed are those who hunger and thirst for righteousness, for they will be filled.

Blessed are the merciful, for they shall obtain mercy.

Blessed are the peacemakers, for they shall be called sons of God. *[God is the supreme peacemaker, and His sons follow His example.]*

Blessed are those who are persecuted for righteousness' sake, for theirs is the kingdom of heaven.

Blessed are you when they revile and persecute you, and say all kinds of evil against you falsely for My sake. Rejoice and be exceedingly glad, for great is your reward in heaven, for so they persecuted the prophets who were before you.

Thus began the Sermon on the Mount, the most-familiar portion of which is the Beatitudes, but it continues with very specific instructions for living a Christian life. If in reading these teachings you feel the pangs of guilt, be comforted by the fact that Jesus took all your sins, past present, and future, upon Himself, leaving your slate absolutely clean when you are spiritually born again. Understand that God does not dwell on your past sins, and neither should you. Believing that, let us continue.

**Believers Are Salt and Light**

> You are the salt of the earth; but if the salt loses its flavor, how shall it be seasoned? It is then good for nothing but to be thrown out and trampled underfoot by men. You are the light of the world. A city that is set on a hill cannot be hidden. Nor do they light a lamp and put it under a basket, but on a lampstand, and it gives light to all who are in the house. Let your light shine before men, that they may see your good works and glorify your

Father in heaven. [*Good deeds for self-glorification are worthless and do not qualify for heavenly reward.*]

## Christ Fulfills the Law

Do not think that I came to destroy the Law or the Prophets. I did not come to destroy but to fulfill. [*He came to fulfill the Old Testament messianic predictions and give the true interpretation to its moral precepts.*]

## Murder Begins in the Heart

You have heard that it is said to those of old, You shall not murder, and whoever murders will be in danger of the judgment. But I say to you that whoever is angry with his brother without cause shall be in danger of the judgment. And whoever says to his brother, "Raca!" shall be in danger of the council. But whoever says, "You fool!" shall be in danger of hell fire. [*Raca is a colloquial expression of contempt for someone's mind, sim-*

*ilar to "blockhead" or "stupid," while fool expresses contempt for someone's character. The both insinuate the person should be doomed to hell.]*

## Adultery in the Heart

> You have heard that it was said to those of old, You shall not commit adultery. But I say to you that whoever looks at a woman to lust for her has already committed adultery in his heart.

## Marriage Is Sacred and Binding

> Furthermore it has been said, Whoever divorces his wife, let him give her a certificate of divorce. But I say to you that whoever divorces his wife for any reason except sexual immorality causes her to commit adultery; and whoever marries a woman who is divorced commits adultery.

## Jesus Forbids Oaths

> You have heard it said to those of old, You shall not swear falsely, but shall perform your oaths to the Lord. But I say to you do not swear at all: neither by heaven, for it is God's throne; nor by earth, for it is His footstool; nor by Jerusalem, for it is the city of the great King. Nor shall you swear by your head, because you cannot make one hair white or black. But let your Yes be Yes and your No, No. For whatever is more than these is from the evil one.

This is by no means the end of the Sermon on the Mount. It continues.

All the time I was writing this, my mind was seeing the mount that overlooks the Sea of Galilee. In 2002 I stood and prayed on the very ground upon which Jesus, my Lord, delivered that sermon. In spite of the fact that I was already saved, that trip where we walked where Jesus walked and baptism in the Jordan River brought a brilliant realism to my faith.

We have a choice—only one. We either live by God's Word here or we don't and spend eternity in torment down there—you know where. So why aren't we all in church on Sunday? I'll give you two reasons: ignorance and pride. There is no excuse for ignorance, and pride is the first of the seven deadly sins. To rid yourself of both, study the Bible. As I said, God did not suggest; He commanded certain behavior. So let's continue the Sermon on the Mount as related in Matthew 5-6.

**Go the Second Mile**

> You have heard that it was said, *An eye for an eye and a tooth for a tooth.* But I tell you not to resist an evil person, but whoever slaps you on the right cheek, turn the other to him also. If anyone want to sue you and take away your tunic, let him have your cloak also. And whoever compels you to go one mile, go with him two. *It was the custom for a Roman soldier on the march to compel a passer bye to carry his load for one mile.*

Give to him who asks you, and from him who wants to borrow from you do not turn away.

## Love Your Enemies

You have heard that it was said, *You shall love your neighbor and hate your enemy.* But I say to you love your enemy, bless those who curse you, do good to those who hate you, and pray for those who spitefully use you and persecute you, that you may be sons of your Father in heaven; for He makes His sun rise on the evil and on the good, and sends rain on the just and on the unjust. For if you love those who love you, what reward have you? Do not even tax collectors do the same? And if you greet your brethren only, what do you do more *than others?* Do not even the tax collectors do so? Therefore you shall be perfect, just as your Father in heaven is perfect.

## Do Good to Please God

> Take heed that you do not do your charitable deeds before men, to be seen by them. Otherwise you have no reward from your Father in heaven. Therefore, when you do a charitable deed, do not sound a trumpet before you as the hypocrites do in the synagogues and in the streets, that they may have glory from men. Assuredly, I say to you, they have their reward. But when you do a charitable deed do not let your left hand know what your right hand is doing, that your charitable deed may be in secret; and your Father who sees in secret will Himself reward you openly.

## The Model Prayer

> And when you pray, you shall not be like the hypocrites. For they love to pray standing in the synagogues and on the street corners, that they may be seen by men. Assuredly, I say to you, they have their reward. But you,

when you pray, go into your room, and when you have shut your door, pray to your Father who is in the secret place; and your Father who sees you in secret will reward you openly.

And when you pray, do not use vain repetitions as the heathens do. For they think that they will be heard for their many words. Therefore do not be like them. For your Father knows the things you have need of before you ask Him. In this manner, therefore, pray:

Our Father in heaven,
Hallowed be you name.
Your kingdom come,
Your will be done
On earth as it is in heaven.
Give us this day our daily bread.
And forgive us our debts,
As we forgive our debtors.
And lead us not into temptation,
But deliver us from the evil one.

> For Yours is the kingdom and the power and the glory forever.
> Amen.
>
> For if you forgive men their trespasses, your heavenly Father will also forgive you. But if you do not forgive men their trespasses, neither will your Father forgive your trespasses.

Continuing the Sermon on the Mount, if we marvel at the changes in lifestyle required to obey God's Word, we can see the extent of our errors and what's needed to correct them. A big change or a little change tells you how far you need to go in your reeducation.

Fasting is giving up something—usually food—that is important to you for a time as a sacrifice to God.

**Fasting to Be Seen Only by God**

> When you fast, keep it a secret between you and God.

**Lay Up Treasures in Heaven**

> Do not lay up for yourselves treasures on earth, where moth and rust destroy and where thieves break in and steal; but lay up for yourselves treasures in heaven, where neither moth nor rust destroys and where thieves do not break in and steal. For where your treasure is, there your heart will be also.

**The Lamp of the Body**

> The lamp of the body is the eye. If therefore your eye is good, your whole body will be full of light. But if your eye is bad, your whole body will be full of darkness, how great is that darkness!

**You Cannot Serve God and Riches**

> No one can serve two masters; for either he will hate the one and love the other, or else he will be loyal to

one and despise other. You cannot serve God and mammon (money).

**Do Not Worry**

Therefore I say to you, do not worry about your life, what you will eat or drink; nor about your body, what you will put on. Is not life more than food and the body more than clothing? Look at the birds of the air, for they neither sow nor reap nor gather into barns; yet your heavenly Father feeds them. Are you not of more value than they? Which of you by worrying can add one cubit to his stature? So why do you worry about clothing? Consider the lilies of the field, how they grow: they neither toil nor spin; and yet I say to you that even Solomon in all his glory was not arrayed like one of these. Now if God so clothed the grass of the field, which today is, and tomorrow is thrown into the oven, will He not much more clothe you, O you of little faith? Therefore do not worry, saying, "What shall we eat?" or

"What shall we drink?" or "what shall we wear?" For after all these things the Gentiles seek. For your heavenly Father knows that you need all these things. But seek first the kingdom of God and His righteousness, and all these things will be added to you. Therefore do not worry about tomorrow, for tomorrow will worry about its own things. Sufficient for the day is its own trouble.

**Do Not Judge**

Judge not that you be not judged. For with what judgment you judge, you will be judged; and with the measure you use, it will be measured back to you. And why do you look at the speck in your brother's eye, but do not consider the plank in your own eye [*finding fault in others when you have plenty of faults on your own*]. Hypocrite! First remove the plank from your own eye, and then you can see clearly to remove the speck from your brother's eye. Do not give what is holy to the dogs; nor cast your pearls before swine, lest they trample them under their feet, and turn and tear you in pieces.

## Keep Asking, Seeking, Knocking

Ask, and it will be given to you; seek, and you will find; knock, and it will be opened to you. For everyone who asks receives, and he who seeks finds, and to him who knocks it will be opened. Or what man is there among you who, if his son asks for bread, will give him a stone? Or if he asks for a fish, will he give him a serpent? If you then, being evil, know how to give good gifts to your children, how much more will your Father who is in heaven give good things to those who ask Him! Therefore, whatever you want men to do to you, do also to them, for this is the Law and the Prophets.

## The Narrow Way

> Enter by the narrow gate; for wide is the gate and broad is the way that leads to destruction, and there are many who go by it. Because narrow is the gate and difficult is the way which leads to life, and there are few who find it.

## You Will Know Them by Their Fruits

> Beware of false prophets, who come to you in sheep's clothing, but inwardly they are ravenous wolves. You will know them by their fruits. Do men gather grapes from thorn bushes or figs from thistles? Even so every good tree bears good fruit, but a bad tree bears bad fruit. A good tree cannot bear bad fruit, nor can a bad tree bear good fruit. Every tree that does not bear good fruit is cut down and thrown into the fire. Therefore by their fruits you will know them.

**I Never Knew You**

> Not everyone who says to me, "Lord, Lord," shall enter the kingdom of heaven, but he who does the will of My Father in heaven. Many will say to Me in that day, "Lord, Lord, have we not prophesied in Your name, cast out demons in Your name, and done many wonders in Your name? And then I will declare to them, "I never knew you; depart from me, you who practice lawlessness!"

**Build on the Rock**

> Therefore whoever hears these words of Mine, and does them, I will liken him to the wise man who built his house on the rock: and the rain descended, the floods came. And the winds blew and beat on that house; and it did not fall, for it was founded on the rock. But everyone who hears these sayings of Mine, and does not do them will be like a foolish man who built his house on sand; and the rain

descended, the floods came, and the winds blew and beat on that house; and it fell. And great was its fall.

And so it was, when Jesus had ended these sayings, that the people were astonished at His teachings, for He taught as one having authority, and not as the scribes.

CHAPTER 5

# A CHRISTIAN WORLD? IT'S COMING WITH JESUS

Of the sixty-six books of the Bible, God used Jews to deliver sixty-four messages to His people. For the other two, God used a gentile doctor named Luke. Being a physician, Luke wrote on a different level than the others, and today the book of Luke and the Acts of the Apostles, simply called the book of Acts, is in popular use today in telling the Jesus story. Although Luke's writing style was different, the facts were as God intended. Using a gentile, God made it plain that the whole world was subject to His commandments, not just the Jews.

God doesn't make bad stuff; He creates works of art. You, my friend, were created as a work of art. However, you permitted the world to make a mess of your life. But hear this: God is not in the business of straightening out your mess. You are a work of art He wants to save.

I've often thought that if all the world had heeded God's Word by putting it into practice, there'd be no such profession as psychology and no psychoanalysis—only reference to God's Word concerning our difficulties. It's already covered, you know. That day is coming when Christ will begin His millennial rule. Imagine if you can a world that is 100 percent Christian, living by God's Law. Paradise. That day will come. That gives us hope, and hope is the secret of life.

What did Jesus say when He healed and forgave? "Go, and sin no more." That will only be possible when Jesus returns; until then, we must try our best not to sin. God will recognize the effort.

The book of Job is generally regarded as the oldest book in the Bible. In it Job declared, "My redeemer lives!" In many other places in the Old Testament prophecy tells of the coming Messiah. Only Jesus fulfilled all the details of all prophesies concerning Him. From the last book of the Old Testament to the birth of Christ, four hundred years elapsed.

Pick up your Bible, hold it to you bosom, and vow to read a chapter a day in preparation for the rapture. There are so many people, but so few will be saved. Be one of them.

## A SENSE OF URGENCY

The world stage is being set for the return of Jesus Christ. If you read the Bible, you know that His return is imminent. Christians will be taken off this earth into the air to join Christ and will avoid the end-time tribulation. We call it the rapture. You cannot work your way to heaven. You need only faith in Jesus Christ to be saved. Without that faith, your "good deeds" are worthless. You may gain recognition and rewards from men, but they mean nothing to God if you don't have faith in His Son. The time is ripe, and tomorrow could be the day of Christ's return. If not then, soon. There will be no warning; be prepared to join Christ when He calls.

Don't exercise your quit option. You are fighting for eternal life in heaven. Are you content to live in hell for all eternity? Or will you fight to be with the Lord in the next life? Then never quit! You must be persuaded that the fight, with all the hardship it entails, is worth it. The heavenly reward is beyond your imagination. I tell you this: if you could imagine only half of what God promises, nothing could make you quit. No hardship, mental or physical, would bring you to the breaking point. Your conviction would be indestructible. You would willingly die rather than deny your faith.

Clinging to this life at the expense of your faith will trash your mansion in heaven. Remember, life is a trial. Heaven is the reward for the winners. Why would you sacrifice heaven with Jesus as your advocate? Jesus is your guarantee. Jesus is your King of Kings and Lord of Lords. Jesus is your answer.

Jesus is your only way to heaven. Jesus is your eternal life. Ignore Him in this life and you've lost it all. Oh, one thing you *will* get is eternal agony and torment as the guest of Satan.

Don't be foolish and gamble that I might be wrong. You will certainly lose your bet.

## ANOTHER WAY OF SAYING IT

Some people say they started to read the Bible but just didn't get it; it seemed so complicated. God gave us four gospels by four different writers so we would be sure to get His simple message. Just so, I've written generally the same message in several articles for the same reason. Just to be sure, let me take another whack at it.

There are so many instances in life that have produced phrases clarifying the situation to man. Many come from the Holy Scriptures, like: *go the extra mile, turn the other cheek, the patience of Job, and that's the cross (burden) I bear,* and many more present-day idioms. There is also a passage in the book of Matthew that describes one's political persuasion as we understand it today. If you are left winger, you are a goat (a liberal) and a right winger a sheep (a conservative, favored by god). Matthew 26:31-35 reads thus:

> But when the Son of Man comes in his glory, and all the angels with him, then he will sit upon his glorious throne. All the nations will be gathered in his presence, and he will separate them as a shepherd separates the sheep from the goats. He will place the sheep at his right hand and the goats at his left. Then the King will say to those on the right, Come, you who are blessed by my father, inherit the Kingdom prepared for you from the foundation of the world. For I was hungry, and you fed me, I was thirsty, and you gave me a drink. I was a stranger, and you invited me into your home.

Whether they understand it or not, liberals make it awfully easy for Satan to do his mischief. Conservatives, at least politically, are more or less on God's side, whether they know it or not. For the conservative, complete faith in God through His Son Jesus is just a short step away. I say, "through Jesus" because God is Spirit. Jesus told us, "If you've seen the Son you've seen the Father." Heaven is His throne, and earth is His footstool. Sounds comfortable, doesn't it? But God left the comfort of heaven and came to earth in the form of man looking for hearts to dwell in, found them, and after taking the burden of their sin and mine to the cross, sent the Holy Spirit to live in our minds and hearts.

God is available to *all* who call on Him, twenty-four/seven. Your sin does not matter; as long as you confess it and ask forgiveness, God will accept you just as you are and transform you into who you should be. Yes, there *are* murderers in heaven who came to know Jesus in this life. There is a praise song we sing in church called "Just as I Am." It goes like this:

> Just as I am without one plea,
> But that Thy blood was shed for me,
> And that thou bidst me come to thee,
> O Lamb of God, I come, I come.

No one's past is so dark that God, in His love, will not forgive you. Say what you will about God or His Son, Jesus, but the Bible tells us that the only unforgivable sin is to blaspheme the Holy Spirit. Webster defines blasphemy thus: "1. Profane abuse of God or sacred things. 2. Anything irreverent."[5]

You are not a Christian unless the Holy Spirit takes up residence in your heart; that is why you must never blaspheme the Holy Spirit. Now, because you received the Holy Spirit, you also accepted Jesus and God because they are one and the same, the Holy Trinity, Father, Son, and the Holy Spirit.

Once again I say that it's not that complicated, is it? When you come to Jesus, your life will change because you want it to. It's like a metamorphosis that changes you from a caterpillar to a butterfly. No change is without struggle, so struggle out of your chrysalis and come fly with Jesus. Just as the emerging butterfly's wings, the struggle will strengthen your character and your faith.

So stop crawling and soar (rise above the ordinary) with Jesus.

---

[5] Ibid. s.v. "blasphemy."

## Common Sense to Nonsense

> On January 9, 1776 Thomas Paine published *Common Sense*, a pamphlet that set the colonies afire with a longing for independence... Paine's words sounded like a trumpet blast through the colonies. Thousands snatched up the pamphlet and decided that he was right. As Thomas Edison, one of America's great geniuses, wrote 150 years later, "We never had a sounder intelligence in this republic..." In *Common Sense* Paine flared forth with a document so powerful that the Revolution became inevitable.
>
> —*The American Patriot's Almanac*[6]

In my day common, sense meant the straight of it—truth and logic. Let me say this—if I have to explain common sense, the country is worse off than I thought.

Describing the hearts of men, the Bible tells us a tree is known by its fruit. Judging by the fruit of an errant administration, we are looking at a socialist tree that is

---

[6] Dr. William Bennett and John T.E. Cribb, *The American Patriot's Almanac*. (Nashville, TN: Thomas Nelson, 2008), 10.

bearing bitter fruit. The land of the free will not endure as the home of the timid and passive.

Cancers start small but will eventually devour the entire body unless a cure is found. In nations the only cure is what the Declaration of Independence states. It is the duty of the people to rise up and replace their government by reasserting the strict interpretation of our divinely inspired Constitution. In 2021 we have the duty as citizens to vote in a new government administration and along with it *term limits to ensure we never come close to destruction again.*

Today our culture has degraded common sense to that which is common in our culture. Therefore, the common sense of my day is uncommon indeed. A great segment of our society can't get through their heads that God's blessings are bestowed on the good. Listen:

> America, America, God shed His grace on thee. And crown thy *good* with brotherhood from sea to shining sea.

America, to me, has always been a magic word full of noble meaning, but in actuality it has lost its shine— not because of her Constitution but because of the bad behavior of her people. We have allowed an immoral minority a platform they don't deserve. Selfish people want more than the Constitution provides. As George Washington said, "The Constitution is a miracle, surely it was written by the finger of God." If so, our immoral minority who want abortion on demand, gay recognition, gay equality, gay marriage, and special rights are, in truth, revolutionaries. This minority and their agenda must not be tolerated in a free society that trusts in God.

Make no mistake about it: God has already begun the end of the world process. He told us to observe the "signs of the times," and they are all around us: a great increase in catastrophic weather phenomenon, rampant increases in pestilence and starvation, frequent earthquakes in diverse places, and moral deterioration. God is shaking us like an unruly child to get our attention and recognize our folly.

There are three things we must do to save ourselves and our nation:

1. We must live by God's law.
2. We must elect to public office men and women who really will defend the Constitution (God's will for our nation).

3. We must become history conscious. History defines us as a people. Our most recent history is shameful.

Now it's up to you to study God's law and live by it. When you have done this, you'll have a great respect not only for our Constitution but for its divine origin as well. It is only common sense to live by our motto: *In God we trust.*

## CHURCH AND STATE

Have you been thinking, *What is this country coming to?* At one time or another we all have. Whatever is wrong with this country is indicative of what's wrong with her people. Their biggest failing is not following directions. Going their own way, they've become lost, floundering around in all directions and nullifying God's plan for their lives. In turning their backs on God, they've turned their backs on their country.

"Separation of church and state" is misunderstood by most. I have made it abundantly clear in previous articles the intent and context of that statement. We are a Christian nation that is tolerant of all religions, but we will not tolerate criticism of ours. The state is responsible for the smooth running of our government. The church is responsible to maintain a high level of morality by means of a Christian education. As a devout Christian, Thomas Jefferson's letter to the clergy made clear that the church need not fear restrictive government policies. The Constitution states that the government may not legislate or discriminate in any way against the church, and the church cannot direct the government. However, Christian education will give us leaders who are both respected by the people and pleasing to God. However, the church *can* and *should* call down the government on moral issues. Lincoln said it, "Nothing is politically correct which is morally wrong."

Our people must have a paradigm shift pertaining to church and state; both are vital to the greatness of America. There is no other way to secure God's blessing on America than for its people to have a healthy respect for both church and state because both are established by God to work together as a team to make a nation great.

In our schools, moral issues must be taught. Moreover, these issues must be tied to the authority of Jesus Christ so as not make them a matter of human choice. I'm talking about obedience to God.

This brings me to "the right to choose," another deceitful expression of our times. An immoral woman chooses who she sleeps with and when she does, and she is choosing the risk of conception. If she becomes pregnant, she has no choice, in God's sight, but to give birth. Abortion is murder. Life begins at conception. We mustn't kid ourselves; Planned Parenthood is a lucrative business no less criminal than "Murder Incorporated" in the eyes of God.

A Christian doctor prayed, "Send someone to cure cancer." God answered, "I did, but you aborted him." You see, when we take the life of an unborn person, we steal a destiny.

Can't you understand why God has poured out adversity on America and the world? He's after our attention. He is shaking the world, and when it seems all is lost, He will return. Be spiritually prepared to meet Jesus face to face. He'll ask, *"What have you done to fit into My plan for your life? Have your pride and ignorance foiled My plan?"*

Can you see now how much easier these issues become from a Christian perspective? *God* is the power. Only your free will can thwart it as it applies to you and your family. God and His people will keep rolling along, leaving you behind to Satan's tender graces.

## CHAPTER 6

# THE TWO-PARTY SYSTEM

People's basic nature is selfish. What's in it for me, and what about me? At election time they focus on current issues in a rather shallow way and don't really appreciate the positions taken by various candidates. The issue's title may sound good, so why is this or that party's candidate against it? In my discussions with people, I've been distressed at their lack of knowledge of the basic tenants of each party. They view only the surface in the form of the person running for office. We must ask ourselves, why is this candidate a Republican or a Democrat? Sometimes I think even the candidates don't know the answer.

What I'm about to describe may sound silly, and I'll admit, it is the result of a rambling imagination, but here goes anyway. Let's look at the symbols adopted by the two parties: the elephant and the jackass.

The elephant has nothing to fear in his world. He is the largest land mammal and is very family oriented and protective. He has no natural enemies. He has attained a certain animal wisdom due to his long memory. In other words, he has learned to appreciate the lessons of his history.

The jackass is defined by Webster in this way: "1) a male donkey 2) a fool."[7] I picture a jackass as sitting on his haunches and refusing to move, stubborn and contrary. Someone help me on this. Are there any characteristics in the jackass that a politician would welcome?

All kidding aside, let's compare the fundamental ideologies of our two parties. First, why are there two parties? Because our founding fathers, in their wisdom, wanted the majority to rule; a third party would split the vote three ways, permitting a victory with less than a majority. In the past a third party has been created to help one of the two parties, who never had a chance of winning, to gain a victory. We must ask: 1) Is the candidate being true to his party's fundamental ideals; 2) What is the difference between the two parties' ideals, and do they apply to the issues?; 3) Does the candidate use only time-tested political rhetoric, or does he have the courage to spell out his plan so the voter can make

---

[7] *Webster's New WorldDictionary,* Fourth Edition, s.v. "jackass."

an intelligent choice?; 4) Most important, does the candidate's background qualify him for this office. Is there a better-qualified man running? Let's compare the fundamentals of each political party.

*The Republican Party* could very accurately be called the Conservative Party. As each of us grows older, in the natural view of things, our experience in life should tend to create a conservative view. Winston Churchill once said, "If by twenty you are not a liberal, you have no heart. If by forty you are not a conservative, you have no brain." That, while witty, is the wisdom of a great leader who understood life's process. Republicans do not believe in "Big Brother" government, which is an all-powerful but an inefficient and wasteful bureaucracy.

Conservative government favors what local governments cannot do for themselves, such as a strong armed forces, a regulated interstate commerce, national parks, national law enforcement to prevent criminals from escaping local justice, and the treasury to protect our currency, to name a few. All of these functions to operate on a tight budget and low federal taxes. This gives local government the responsibility to levy taxes for such things as public schools and infrastructure. The experience prepares locally elected officials for higher office, hopefully for limited terms. This gives local government back to the people, where it belongs, with no federal strings attached. Conservatives believe we must get out from under the big club of a monstrous bureaucracy that dictates to local government and withholds funds if they don't fall in line.

The smaller the government structure, the more talented government employees. A massive federal bureaucracy attracts mediocrity. The bigger the government, the easier it is for the unqualified or lazy to hide in its bureaucratic bowels. Conservatives tend to eliminate restrictive policies that inhibit private industry and depress the economy. After all, private enterprise is by far our biggest employer. Healthy businesses create a healthy economy.

*The Democratic Party* could be called the Liberal Party. This party has become one most clear-thinking conservatives have outgrown, and it is a party that leans heavily toward socialism. They know human nature and cater to the voters' selfishness. By discussing what conservatives are against, we find what liberals are for; big government with big, money-sucking programs that take us to socialism, where the people have lost control and many of their freedoms.

Liberals tend to tread on the morals of the nation. The best thing the democrats have done, in more conservative times, is to protect the elderly with social security and Medicare, which the elderly paid for in their productive years. That is the way the Roosevelt administration saw it—a trust fund paid into by the workers for income in the days when they could no longer work. But as time marched on, the congress violated that trust by repeated raiding of the fund and promising to pay it back, but it never did—not once. Now they have the gall to say it has run out of money. The Roosevelt administration should have made it illegal to dip into the fund, but it has become a slush fund for professional politicians.

Let's not get any closer to socialism; when we do, we are letting the government become all things to all men, and friends, that's *expensive*! It will rob you of income and freedom. Democrats are throwing away money to illegal aliens, failing to enforce immigration laws, and considering amnesty to broaden their voter base. At this rate, soon there will be no advantage to being a legal citizen. The Democrats have outgrown their validity as the party of the people and have become the party of career politicians who are working for themselves. Their tax-and-spend philosophy to maintain power has only hurt the economy and the people and weakened the people's faith in God.

It is no surprise that I am a republican, proud to say so, and at ninety years young, I've seen enough to be staunchly conservative, and so, the Bible tells me, is God. It's a comfortable feeling to know that I am on God's side.

Things have gone too far for Band-Aids. The certain way to correct the situation and bring validity back to the Democratic Party is a constitutional amendment to limit terms of office, just as was envisioned by our founding fathers. This will give the voters the power, not professional politicians looking for personal gain.

## USA OR DSA?

There used to appear on our currency *E. Pluribus Unum (the many are one).* Where did it go? Could it be that we are admitting that we are no longer united? Perhaps we should change our name from the United States of America to the Divided States of America. Not since the Civil War has our country been so polarized. Liberals and conservatives are so far apart that compromise is not acceptable to either side. Compromise keeps us on an even keel and prevents extremism.

Look at it this way: conservatives drive in the right lane at or below the speed limit, within the spirit of the law. Liberals drive in the left lane, exceeding the speed limit, and think they are the law unto themselves, pushing the law as far as they think their brand of freedom will allow. They are encouraged by liberal organizations with innocent-sounding names like Planned Parenthood, the murder mill for unwanted pregnancies, and the American Civil Liberties Union, which supports homosexuality and an extreme liberal agenda, including the suppression of freedom of worship.

Extreme liberals hold a mistaken view of freedom as their god, when in fact they are blind to the ultimate authority in life—almighty God. Liberalism shows in attitude, business dealings, and politics that we have, as a nation, drifted into an immoral lifestyle. It has come so far that liberals call conservatives extremists. We call bad good and good bad. Is it any wonder we are the divided states of America?

The Bible tells of kingdoms God has given over to depravity and allowed them to destroy themselves. Miss Liberty is weeping because she has been raped by liberal extremists. Her light has gone out. We must waste no time rekindling that light for all the world to see.

So what can bring us together? The answer is on our coins to remind us: *in God we trust.* We must be true to our motto. It must have meaning by putting God back in His rightful place—the public classroom.

Nothing will reunite our ailing country like a Christian education administered with love and compassion. The Holy Scriptures are God's voice. Listen to Him and you will prosper in ways you never dreamed.

## FREE WILL

Is free will a gift or a curse? God gave it to you. Now it's squarely up to you what you do with it. Free will means choices, good or bad, wise or ignorant, calculated or emotional. Yes, free will is a gift from God; it makes us the highest form of life. Animals and birds are given the gift of instinct for survival, but they don't reason. Knowing all this, each of us are responsible for living our lives well, but only those who are aware of God's will can live it really well.

Where we run into real trouble is when we let emotions rule. Depression, anger, love, hate, fear, and pride can cause us to make disastrous choices that can ruin our finances, relationships, and golf game. Very few folks who take up the game play golf strictly by the rules, so they are cheaters. But we all cheat at the game of life. The greatest trick the Devil ever pulled was convincing the world he doesn't exist.

Looking around, we might think life is heavily loaded in Satan's favor and we exercise our free will accordingly, sentencing ourselves to hell in the process. But God has the great counterbalance: forgiveness for those who ask. They ask because they have become aware of God's will by means of a Christian education. God has the capacity not only to forgive sin but also forget sins, as if they never happened, leaving you with a clean slate, a chance to begin again. Haven't you ever wished that something you did had never happened? Well, God provides the only way that can happen through His forgiveness. Yes, there are ex-criminals in heaven because God can change anyone and does, every day.

My church is large. The sanctuary holds thirteen hundred people and requires three morning services to minister to overflow crowds. Within the church there are many small groups that meet regularly, targeting every human frailty imaginable. People are anxious to tell their personal stories of salvation—stories about Jesus on demand.

Yes, your free will comes from God; how to best use it also comes from God and requires a Christian education to work for your benefit.

## THE END OF THE BOOK

Some might say Revelation is the end of the Bible, but I see it as the beginning of eternal life. It is the believer's springboard to heaven because it tells us about events only atheists and agnostics will suffer. The book of Revelation is full of symbolism and can be difficult to understand, even if you've read the rest of the Bible. Revelation was written by John around AD 94 to 96. He was the last survivor of the original twelve disciples and had been banished by Rome to the island of Patmos for his vigorous preaching of the gospel. The island is located off the coast of Turkey, then known as Asia Minor, opposite Ephesus on the Aegean Sea. There John received a series of visions that described the future of the world. The visions revealed Jesus Christ as the divine Shepherd who is concerned about the condition of the church. He told John to write letters to the seven churches of Asia Minor.

Here I will confine my discussion to chapters 2 and 3 of Revelation. In the letters, Jesus, after some compliments, pointed out their errors. Because these errors are still with us today, I'll list them:

Church #1: The loveless church—Ephesus: "You have lost your first love" (2:4).

Church #2: The persecuted church—Smyrna: "I know how much you have suffered" (2:9).

Church #3: The lax church—Pergamos: "You tolerate sin" (2:14-15).

Church #4: The compromising church—Thyatira: "You permit the teaching of immoral practices" (2:20).

Church #5: The lifeless church—Sardis: "You are dead" (3:1).

Church # 6: The obedient church—Philadelphia: "You have...kept My word, and have not denied My name" (3:8).

Church # 7: The lukewarm church—Laodicea: "You are neither hot nor cold" (3:15).

Think—have you drifted away and forgotten God; are you hot or cold, dead, tolerant of sin; do you permit the teaching of immoral practices such as "alternate lifestyles" in our schools? Finally, has your school banned the mention of God by teachers, or do they teach the truth? What is truth? That which agrees with the Word of God is truth; contradiction is a lie.

These and other questions are answered in the last book of the Bible, Revelation. It also tells us what the wrath of God will bring to those who have no faith or believe false prophets.

Today in some of the world, Christians are being summarily executed for their faith; possession of a Bible is all it takes. The same will happen here during the seven-year reign of the antichrist when there is only one world religion with its false prophet. The antichrist will demand what Satan has always wanted: to be worshiped as a deity. The false prophet will pronounce him god. I tell you this: you don't want to be here during the reign of the antichrist. You have your warning in the book of Revelation.

Let me close with this: it is quite possible for a Bible scholar to know the Bible but not believe it in his or her heart. These are people who treat the ministry as a job but don't really believe what they teach. God knows your heart. These people will fare no better than the agnostic or the atheist on judgment day. To know is one thing; to believe is another.

A well-known celebrity once said, "Only I can change my life. No one can do it for me." Oh? I suppose that's true in its context; she must make the decision to change. But as a Christian, I would put it this way: "Only I can stop struggling and let God change my life; He controls it anyway."

# CHAPTER 7

# MORAL COURAGE

It is unfathomable that Americans are apologizing for who we are. This is the attitude that toppled us from our place at the top of the list of nations. It rankles me that we tolerate anything for fear we will *offend* some individual or culture. Who cares if the truth offends the liar? What I am about to suggest is considered by professional politicians to be political suicide, but it is a fact that must be exposed to the light of day for all to understand. The last virtue of a decadent society is *tolerance*. We are bending over backward to tolerate immorality in just about all its forms. Political moral courage is nearly nonexistent, but apparently not in Australia. Former Prime Minister John Howard told Muslims who want to live under Islamic Sharia law to get out of Australia as the government targeted radicals in a bid to head off potential terror attacks. In quoting Mr. Howard, I have substituted *two terms* to bring home what must be done here: *America and the World Trade Center.*

*Immigrants, not Americans, must adapt.* Take it or leave it. I am tired of this nation worrying about whether we are offending some individual or their culture. Since the terrorist attack on the World Trade Center, we have experienced a surge in patriotism by the majority of Americans. This culture has been developed over three centuries of struggle, trials and victories, by millions of men and women who have sought freedom.

We speak *English*, not Spanish, Lebanese, Arabic, Chinese, Russian, or any other language. Therefore, if you wish to become part of our society, learn the language!

Most Americans believe in God. This is not some Christian, right wing, political push, but a fact, because Christian men and women, on Christian principles founded this nation, and this is clearly documented. It's certainly appropriate to display it on the walls of our schools. If God offends you, then I suggest you consider another part of the world as your new home, because God is part of our culture. We will accept your beliefs, and will not question why. All we ask is that you accept ours, and live in harmony and peaceful enjoyment with us.

This is *our country, our land*, and *our lifestyle*, and we will allow you every opportunity to enjoy all of this. But once you are done complaining, whining, and griping About Our Flag, Our Pledge, Our Christian beliefs, or Our Way of life, I highly encourage you take advantage of one other great American freedom, *the right to leave.*

If you aren't happy here then *leave*. We didn't force you to come here. You asked to be here. So accept the country *you* accepted.

We must take back our country from the extreme left. Conservatives are not flashy. They don't make a lot of noise, but they will quietly put our country back on its feet and continue to pursue freedom and prosperity for all. That's the American way.

What we need is a *president* with the moral and political courage to *lead*, and to shout, "Damn political correctness!" and do what is morally right. Americans will respect that kind of courage. I can't see that coming from this president (Biden) but I fervently hope it will come from the next, who will most likely offend the liars. Let us not let the tail wag the dog. The last virtue of a decadent society is tolerance. We are bending over backward to tolerate immorality of nearly all sorts.

*Come on, man!*

## A GOOD MAN

You've probably heard, "A good man nowadays is hard to find." I ask you, why should that be the case? Looking back at the history of our nation, men who left their mark were good, God-fearing men who didn't need courage to stand for Christ; so why does it take courage to take that stand today? It takes true conviction to speak publicly about one's faith in today's world. Why again? Because our society has sunk so low that it is not considered politically correct to teach the Bible in our schools.

Our children have grown up separated from God, and our nation has suffered the consequences: corruption in high places, loss of individual integrity, businesses that put the bottom line before human considerations, crooked politicians, and a terribly high crime rate, filling our prisons to overflowing at a cost we can ill afford. Where are the good men? Today they are harder to find than ever, and when you find one, he doesn't want to be stained by the label "politician." We desperately need a generation of statesmen.

If you are a regular reader of my blogs, you may wonder why I've quoted Abraham Lincoln, a Republican, so often. It's because he was a good, honest, God-fearing man, educated in the Bible. His eloquent words ring in our ears today as the most quoted in a long line of chief executives. Until we put the Bible in its rightful place in our public schools and raise a new crop of good, God-fearing statesmen, it's best not to put young men in high office. America needs to outgrow the sins of the past by inviting God back into our lives.

On March 30, 1863 (in the midst of the Civil War), President Abraham Lincoln issued a historic *Proclamation Appointing a National Fast Day.*

Whereas, the Senate of the United States devoutly recognizing the Supreme Authority and just Government of Almighty God in all the affairs of men and of nations, has, by a resolution requested the President to designate and set apart a day for national prayer and humiliation:

And whereas, it is the duty of nations as well as of men to owe their dependence upon the overruling power of God, to confess their sins and transgressions in humble sorrow yet with assured hope that genuine repentance will lead to mercy and pardon, and to recognize the sublime truth, announced in the Holy Scriptures and proven by all history: that those nations only are blessed whose God is Lord:

And, insomuch as we know that, by His divine law, nations like individuals are subjected to punishments and chastisement in this world, may we not justly fear that the awful calamity of civil war, which now desolates the land may be but a punishment inflicted upon us for our presumptuous sins to the needful end of our national reformation as a whole people?

We have been the recipients of the choicest bounties of Heaven. We have been preserved these many years in peace and prosperity. We have grown in numbers, wealth and power as no other nation has ever grown.

But we have forgotten God. We have forgotten the gracious Hand which preserved us in peace, and multiplied and enriched and strengthened us; and we have vainly imagined, in the deceitfulness of our hearts, that all these blessings were produced by some superior wisdom and virtue of our own.

Intoxicated with unbroken success, we have become too selfsufficient to feel the necessity of redeeming and preserving grace, too proud to pray to the God that made us!

It behooves us then to humble ourselves before the offended Power, to confess our national sins and to pray for clemency and forgiveness.

Now, therefore, in compliance with the request and fully concurring in the view of the Senate, I do, by this my proclamation, designate and set apart Thursday, the 30$^{th}$ day of April, 1863, as a day of national humiliation, fasting and prayer.

> And I do hereby request all the people to abstain on that day from their ordinary secular pursuits, and unite, at their several places of public worship and their respective homes, in keeping the day holy to the Lord and devoted to the humble discharge of religious duties proper to that solemn occasion.
>
> All this being done, in sincerity and truth, let us then rest humbly in the hope authorized by Divine teachings, that the united cry of the nation will be heard on high and answered with blessing no less than the pardon of our national sins and the restoration of our now divided and suffering country to its former happy condition of unity and peace.

Those are the words of Honest Abe.

Today we are just as divided as the South was from the North, only now the two factions are those who stand for Christ and those who won't. Those who won't today are just as guilty as those who practiced slavery then. Every man, woman, and child must get it into our heads and hearts that we are, on purpose, a Christian nation. Now where is the good, God-fearing man who can lead our nation to a new and holy union?

## CONGRESSIONAL REFORM

Pastors should not meddle in politics. However, as the Lord's ambassadors, the church must call down anyone or any department in the government on moral issues because we are a Christian nation—a fact substantiated by the Supreme Court many times in announcing the results of their deliberations. Our major problem is the power-hungry professional politicians and the way they run the congress to suit themselves.

For months I have been telling you about the failings of congress. I don't propose to repeat myself here except to say that congress has grossly distorted the intent of our founding fathers. Signers of our God-given Constitution would be shocked and horrified at the unintended power and special privileges that professional politicians have bestowed upon themselves without the approval of the people.

To correct this injustice, the people *must* apply pressure to reform the way congress conducts the people's business.

**Subject:** The Congressional Reform Act of 2013

Warren Buffett, in a recent interview with CNBC, offers one of the best quotes about the debt ceiling: "I could end the deficit in five minutes," he told CNBC. "You just pass a law that says that anytime there is a deficit of more than 3 percent of GDP, all sitting members of Congress are ineligible for re-election."

The twenty-sixth amendment (granting the right to vote for eighteen-year-olds) took only three months and eight days to be ratified! Why? Simple! The people demanded it. That was in 1971—before computers, e-mail, cell phones, etc.

Of the twenty-seven amendments to the Constitution, seven took one year or less to become the law of the land…all because of public pressure.

## The Congressional Reform Act must include:

1. No tenure/establishing term limits. Congressmen will collect a salary while in office and will receive no pay when they are out of office.

2. Congress (past, present, and future) must participate in Social Security. All funds in the congressional retirement fund will be moved to the Social Security system immediately. All future funds must flow into the Social Security system, and congress must participate with the American people. It may not be used for any other purpose.

3. Congress can purchase their own retirement plan, just as all Americans do.

4. Congress will no longer vote themselves a pay raise. Congressional pay will rise by the CPI or 3 percent, whichever is lower.

5. Congress will end their current health-care system and participate in the same health-care system as the American people.

6. Congress must equally abide by all laws they impose on the American people.

7. All contracts with past and present Congressmen are void effective upon radification. The American people did not make this contract with congressmen. Congressmen made all these contracts for themselves. *Serving in congress is an honor, not a career.* The founding fathers envisioned citizen legislators, so ours should serve their limited term(s) and then go home and back to work.

This'll fix it.

## CITIZENSHIP

Your citizenship in a free America is not free; it is something to be treasured and guarded with your life against all enemies, foreign and domestic (enemies from without and enemies from within). What kind of citizen does God expect us to be?

Matthew 17:24-27 says, "However, we don't want to offend them, so go down to the lake and throw in a line. Open the mouth of the first fish you catch, and you will find a coin. Take the coin and pay the tax for both of us."

*"Christians are required to be responsible citizens.*

As God's people, we are foreigners on earth because our real home is in heaven. Still we have to cooperate with the authorities and be responsible citizens. An ambassador to another country keeps the local laws in order to represent well the one who sent him. We are Christ's ambassadors (2 Cor. 5:20). Are you being a good foreign ambassador for Him to this country?

Romans 13:1-14 says, "Obey the government, for God is the one who put it there. All governments have been placed in power by God."

*Christians are required to take their earthly citizenship very seriously.*

Christians understand Romans 13 in different ways. All Christians agree that we are to live in peace with the state as long as the state allows us to live by our religious convictions. For hundreds of years, however, there have been at least three interpretations of how we are to do this.

1. Some Christians believe that the state is so corrupt that Christians should have as little to do with it as possible. Although they should be good citizens as long as they can do so without compromising their beliefs, they should

not work for the government, vote, or serve in the military.
2. Others believe that God has given the state authority in certain areas and the church authority in others. Christians can be loyal to both and can work for either. They should not, however, confuse the two. In this view, church and state are concerned with two totally different spheres—the spiritual and the physical—and thus complement each other but do not work together.
3. Still others believe that Christians have a responsibility to make the state better. They can also do this morally, serving as an influence for good in society. In this view, church and state ideally work together for the good of all.

None of these views advocate rebelling against or refusing to obey the government's laws or regulations unless they clearly require you to violate the moral standards revealed by God. Wherever we find ourselves, we must be responsible citizens as well as responsible Christians."

The above is an excerpt from a wonderfully presented and educational book covering all questions you may have just by going to the appropriate word, in this case *citizenship*. We have in previous articles spoken of our responsibilities as earthly citizens and in particular, US citizens. When we misbehave, we will be called to account and receive our just punishment under the law. The Bible teaches we must face God's judgment, but as believers we have settled out of court. What better advocate could we have than the Son of the Judge—the Lamb of God?

*What are the benefits of being a citizen of God's Kingdom?*

Revelation 21:15-27 says: "Nothing evil will be allowed to enter—no one who practices shameful idolatry and dishonesty—but only those whose names are written in the Lamb's Book of Life."

Citizenship in God's kingdom brings eternal benefits. Not everyone will be allowed into the New Jerusalem, "only those whose names are written in the Lamb's Book of Life." Don't think that you will get in because of your background, personality, or good behavior. Eternal life is available to you only because of what Jesus, the Lamb, has done. Trust Him today to secure your citizenship in His new creation.

Colossians 1:13-14 says: "For he has rescued us from the one who rules in the kingdom of darkness, and he has brought us into the Kingdom of his dear Son. God has purchased our freedom with his blood and has forgiven all our sins."

Citizenship in God's kingdom brings immediate benefits. Paul lists five benefits God gives all believers through Christ: (1) He made us qualified to share His inheritance; (2) He rescued us from Satan's domination of darkness and made us His children; (3) He brought us into His eternal kingdom; (4) He redeemed us—bought our freedom from sin and judgment; and (5) He forgave all our sins. Thank God for what you have received in Christ. (Handbook of Bible Application. Neil S. Wilson, Editor, Tyndale House Publishers, Inc.

## CHAPTER 8

# INDEPENDENCE DAY

When I asked a young middle schooler the significance of the Fourth of July, her answer was, "It's fireworks day." I pressed for a better answer, and the child looked at me like I didn't know myself and shrugging her shoulders, gave no answer. Isn't that a shame? Her response is an indictment of our education system.

The holiday does not celebrate our Constitution but our Declaration of Independence from Great Britain as represented by the tyrant King George III. Today there is much discussion about the Constitution, but in our secular society, the Declaration of Independence has been put on the back shelf because it has too many references to God in its text—yes, and for no other reason. The 244 years of our existence as a nation are dated from the signing of the Declaration of Independence, and yet, the two documents must be considered as equally essential to the birth of our nation.

Allow me to compare the birth of our nation with the birth of a corporation. Establishing a corporation requires composing the articles of incorporation (the aims and purpose of the corporation) and the bylaws, which implement the methods to accomplish the aims and purpose of the firm. So the Declaration of Independence, with its twenty-seven grievances against the king, is our articles of incorporation, and the Constitution is our bylaws, which lay out our method of accomplishment. The two cannot be separated. Let me insert here what President George Washington said about the Constitution, "It is a miracle...surely it was written by the finger of God." And John Jay said, "Every citizen should read and study the Constitution; it is a godly document."

So we are celebrating our separation from England and the birthday of our nation on this fourth day of July. It is also essential for us to understand why it was necessary to sever our ties to England. The best answer to that question is the Declaration of Independence itself.

When in the Course of human events, it becomes necessary for one people to dissolve the political bands which have connected them with another, and to assume among the powers of the earth, the separate and equal station to which the Laws of Nature and of

Nature's God entitle them, a decent respect to the opinions of mankind requires that they should declare the causes which impel them to the separation.

We hold these truths to be self-evident, that all men are created equal, that they are endowed by their Creator with certain unalienable Rights, that among these are Life, Liberty and the pursuit of Happiness. That to secure these rights, Governments are instituted among Men, deriving their just powers from the consent of the governed, that whenever any Form of Government becomes destructive of these ends, it is the Right of the People to alter or to abolish it, and to institute new Government, laying its foundation on such principles and organizing its powers in such form, as to them shall seem most likely to effect their Safety and Happiness. Prudence, indeed, will dictate that Governments long established should not be changed for light and transient causes; and accordingly all experience hath shewn, that mankind are more disposed to suffer, while evils are sufferable, than to right themselves by abolishing the forms to which they are accustomed. But when a long train of abuses and usurpations, pursuing invariably the same Object evinces a design to reduce them under absolute Despotism, it is their right, it is their duty, to throw off such Government, and to provide new Guards for their future security.

The next section is a list of charges against King George III, which aim to demonstrate that he has violated the colonists' rights and is therefore unfit to be their ruler.

> Such has been the patient sufferance of these Colonies; and such is now the necessity which constrains them to alter their former Systems of Government. The history of the present King of Great Britain is a history of repeated injuries and usurpations, all having in direct object the establishment of an absolute Tyranny over these States. To prove this, let Facts be submitted to a candid world.
>
> He has refused his Assent to Laws, the most wholesome and necessary for the public good.
>
> He has forbidden his Governors to pass Laws of immediate and pressing importance, unless suspended in their operation till his Assent should be obtained; and when so suspended, he has utterly neglected to attend to them.

He has refused to pass other Laws for the accommodation of large districts of people, unless those people would relinquish the right of Representation in the Legislature, a right inestimable to them and formidable to tyrants only.

He has called together legislative bodies at places unusual, uncomfortable, and distant from the depository of their public Records, for the sole purpose of fatiguing them into compliance with his measures.

He has dissolved Representative Houses repeatedly, for opposing with manly firmness his invasions on the rights of the people.

He has refused for along time, after such dissolutions, to cause others to be elected; whereby the Legislative powers, incapable of Annihilation, have returned to the People at large for their exercise; the State remaining in the meantime exposed to all the dangers of invasion from without, and convulsions within.

He has endeavoured to prevent the population of these States; for that purpose obstructing the Laws for Naturalization of Foreigners; refusing to pass others to encourage their migrations hither, and raising the conditions of new Appropriations of Lands.

He has obstructed the Administration of Justice, by refusing his Assent to Laws for establishing Judiciary powers.

He has made Judges dependent on his Will alone, for the tenure of their offices, and the amount and payment of their salaries.

He has erected a multitude of New Offices, and sent hither swarms of Officers to harass our people, and eat out their substance.

He has kept among us, in times of peace, Standing Armies without the Consent of our legislatures.

He has affected to render the Military independent of and superior to the Civil power.

He has combined with others to subject us to a jurisdiction foreign to our constitution, and unacknowledged by our laws; giving his Assent to their Acts of pretended Legislation:

For Quartering large bodies of armed troops among us:

For protecting them, by a mock Trial, from punishment for any Murders which they should commit on the Inhabitants of these States:

For cutting off our Trade with all parts of the world:

For imposing Taxes on us without our Consent:

For depriving us in many cases, of the benefits of Trial by Jury:

For transporting us beyond Seas to be tried for pretended offences

For abolishing the free System of English Laws in a neighbouring Province, establishing therein an Arbitrary government, and enlarging its Boundaries so as to render it at once an example and fit instrument for introducing the same absolute rule into these Colonies:

For taking away our Charters, abolishing our most valuable Laws, and altering fundamentally the Forms of our Governments:

For suspending our own Legislatures, and declaring themselves invested with power to legislate for us in all cases whatsoever.

He has abdicated Government here, by declaring us out of his Protection and waging War against us.

He has plundered our seas, ravaged our Coasts, burnt our towns, and destroyed the lives of our people.

He is at this time transporting large Armies of foreign Mercenaries to compleat the works of death, desolation and tyranny, already begun with circumstances of Cruelty & perfidy scarcely paralleled in the most barbarous ages, and totally unworthy the Head of a civilized nation.

He has constrained our fellow Citizens taken Captive on the high Seas to bear Arms against their Country, to become the executioners of their friends and Brethren, or to fall themselves by their Hands.

He has excited domestic insurrections amongst us, and has endeavoured to bring on the inhabitants of our frontiers, the merciless Indian Savages, whose known rule of warfare, is an undistinguished destruction of all ages, sexes and conditions.

In every stage of these Oppressions We have Petitioned for Redress in the most humble terms: Our repeated Petitions have been answered only by repeated injury. A Prince whose character is thus marked by every act which may define a Tyrant, is unfit to be the ruler of a free people. Nor have we been wanting in attentions to our British brethren. We have warned them from time to time of attempts by their legislature to extend an unwarrantable jurisdiction over us. We have reminded them of the circumstances of our emigration and settlement here. We have appealed to their native justice and magnanimity, and we have conjured them by the ties of our common kindred to disavow these usurpations, which, would inevitably interrupt our connections and correspondence. They too have been deaf to the voice of justice and of consanguinity. We must, therefore, acquiesce in the necessity, which denounces our Separation, and hold them, as we hold the rest of mankind, Enemies in War, in Peace Friends.

We, therefore, the Representatives of the united States of America, in General Congress, Assembled, appealing to the Supreme Judge of the world for the rectitude of our intentions, do, in the Name, and by Authority of the good People of these Colonies, solemnly publish and declare, That these United Colonies are, and of Right ought to be Free and Independent States; that they are Absolved from all Allegiance to the British Crown, and that all political connection between them and the State of Great Britain, is and ought to be totally dissolved; and that as Free and Independent States, they have full Power to levy War, conclude Peace, contract Alliances, establish

Commerce, and to do all other Acts and Things which Independent States may of right do. And for the support of this Declaration, with a firm reliance on the protection of divine Providence, we mutually pledge to each other our Lives, our Fortunes and our sacred Honor.

## CHAPTER 9

# THE BILL OF RIGHTS

We don't claim our Constitution to be a perfect document. After the Constitutional Convention of 1787, some delegates felt the Constitution didn't include enough safeguards to protect the individual freedoms, so they refused to sign it. The same problem surfaced during the ratification process. In 1789 James Madison (who would become the fourth president) led the effort to write amendments spelling out basic rights. Today we have twenty-seven amendments to the Constitution, the first ten of which are known as the Bill of Rights.

Article V of the Constitution states,

> The Congress, whenever two thirds of both Houses shall deem it necessary, shall propose Amendments to this Constitution, or, on the Application of the Legislatures of two thirds of

several States, shall call a Convention for proposing amendments, which, in either Case, shall be valid to all Intents and Purposes, as Part of this Constitution when ratified by the Legislatures of three fourths of the several States, or by Conventions in three fourths thereof, as the one or the other Mode or Ratification may be proposed by Congress; Provided that no Amendment which may be made prior to the Year One thousand eight hundred and eight shall in any manner affect the first and fourth Clauses in the Ninth Section of the Article; and that no State, without its consent, shall be deprived of its equal Suffrage in the Senate.

So no tyrant can change a word of our Constitution. The power remains in the hands of the people. Do we deserve it? Nikita Kruschev, former chairman of the Soviet Union, speaking to the United States declared, "Give me one generation and we will bury you." We don't appreciate how close he came to making good on that statement. Our public education system, whether it knew it or not, was setting us up for just that. Thank

God for a president with the courage to call the Soviets' hand. Now we are still left with a generation without faith. We must correct that situation by returning the Holy Bible not only to the public classroom but also to the media. God is blessing the faithful, but we need His blessing on our nation.

That said, let's read, for the first time for many of us, the first ten amendments to the Constitution—the Bill of Rights.

> Amendment I
> Congress shall make no law respecting an establishment of religion, or prohibiting the free exercise thereof; or abridging the freedom of speech, or of the press; or the right of the people peaceably to assemble, and to petition the Government for a redress of grievances.
>
> Amendment II
> A well regulated Militia, being necessary to the security of a free State, the right of the people to keep and bear Arms, shall not be infringed.

Amendment III

No soldier shall, in time of peace be quartered in any house, without the consent of the Owner, nor in time of war, but in a manner to be prescribed by law.

Amendment IV

The right of the people to be secure in their persons, houses, papers and effects, against unreasonable searches and seizures, shall not be violated, and no Warrants shall issue, but upon probable cause, supported by Oath or affirmation, and particularly describing the place to be searched, and the persons or things to be seized.

Amendment V

No person shall be held to answer of a capital, or otherwise infamous crime, unless on a presentment or indictment of a Grand Jury, except in cases arising in the land or naval forces, or in the militia, when in actual service in time of War or public danger; nor shall any person be subject for the same offence to be twice put in jeopardy on life or limb; nor shall be compelled in any criminal case to be a witness against himself; nor be deprived of life, liberty, or property, without due process of law; nor shall private property be taken for public use, without just compensation.

Amendment VI
In all criminal prosecutions the accused shall enjoy the right to a speedy and public trial, by an impartial jury of the State and district wherein the crime shall have been committed, which district shall have been previously ascertained by law, and to be informed of the nature and cause of the accusation; to be confronted with witnesses against him, to have compulsory process for obtaining witnesses in his favor, and to have the Assistance of Counsel for his defense.

Amendment VII

In suits at common law, where the value in controversy shall exceed twenty dollars, the right of trial by jury shall be preserved, and no fact tried by jury, shall be otherwise re-examined in any court of the United States, than according to the rules of the common law.

Amendment VIII

Excessive bail shall not be required, nor excessive fines imposed, nor cruel and unusual punishments inflicted.

Amendment IX

The enumeration in the Constitution of certain rights, shall not be construed to deny or disparage others retained by the people.

Amendment X

The powers not delegated to the United States by the Constitution, nor prohibited by it to the States, are reserved to the States respectively, or to the people.

Over the years, seventeen additional amendments were added, excepting one that was repealed not only because it didn't work but because it created organized crime syndicates in America—Prohibition. Yes, our mistakes can be corrected lawfully by the will of the people. We are a nation of laws. We should never pass a law we are not ready and able to enforce; that includes our immigration law, which establishes annual quotas for various countries. Also, currently some states are preparing for a constitutional convention to establish term limits for representatives and senators to remedy what our wise founding fathers feared: the career politician. Please support this effort by writing or calling your own senator and representative. This will make our system work.

CHAPTER 10

# PHYSICAL AND SPIRITUAL BALANCE = WELL BEING

You may be the finest physical specimen on the block, but if your spirit is sick sooner or later your physical health will suffer. You must have balance. You've heard the question, "Why does a loving God send people to hell?" The truth is He doesn't. God values freedom so he gave man a free will. Man chooses hell by not choosing God through Jesus Christ. Jesus told us, in no uncertain terms, "I am the way, the truth and the life. No one comes to the Father except by me" (John 14:6) and "You are either for me or against me" (Matt. 12:30).

Understand this: without the *way*, there is no going, without the *truth*, there is no knowing, and without the *life*, there is no living. There is no fence sitting, no middle ground because doubt is Satan's playground. The Lord also said, "Would that you be hot or cold, but because you are lukewarm I'll spew you out of my mouth" (Rev. 3:16). John 3:16 says, "God so loved the world that He gave His only begotten son that whosoever believes in Him shall not perish but have everlasting life." God's plan for your life is simple; people complicate it by trying to reinvent the wheel. Would you rather drag yourself through life or ride on wheels? Let your stumbling block be a stepping stone to a higher level in your life. What do you think life is for if not to make the ultimate choice?

God's Word is the ultimate truth by which we should all be living; truth is that which agrees with the Word of God. But no, by choice, worldly men and women have placed themselves above God; they believe they have a better idea and just look at this sinful world in chaos. Just like the Israelites of ancient days, man has written millions of laws covering every human aspect of life. It's ridiculous that it has now become impossible to live without breaking some obscure, unenforceable law—laws that are already covered in spirit by the law of God, the Ten Commandments. If a nation and its people observed the spirit of God's law, all the law books in every lawyer's office would be reduced to one page upon which was written the Ten Commandments.

Look at a world of a poverty of spirit living a lie and destined for hell. Turn your back on the world, run to the loving arms of Jesus your Savior, and accept the free gift of citizenship in heaven and you will find love and peace in your spirit that will transform your being. Jesus said, "My yoke is easy and my burden is light" (Matt. 11:30). Don't ignore the truth; embrace it. The alternative is a lie, and the consequence is eternity in torment. Jesus also said "I have come to give testimony to the truth" (John 8:14). I believe Jesus is capable of telling only the truth. He told us, "When you've seen me you've seen the Father" (John 14:9). I believe He is who He says He is—the Son of God.

I have used the present tense because Jesus is eternal and is alive today in the heart of everyone who is born again. Christianity is all about beginning again with a clean slate. What price would you pay to be safe, secure, and prosperous? Accepting salvation is easy, but living out a Christian life in this sinful world is not but so worth the effort. He told us He was sending us out like sheep among wolves. Yes, the easy part is to believe in the Lord Jesus and you will be saved. Saved from what? Hell. You are saved for God. Now He says we must sin no more. He put you on this earth, and He expects to bring you home. Please, don't disappoint Him.

Let me ask you this: Is your car insured? Do you believe you will have an accident? Is your life insured? Do you believe you will die prematurely? Then by insuring, you are playing it safe, right? You may not believe in life after death either, but suppose you are wrong—and there is plenty of evidence you would be. Shouldn't you take out some insurance? The biggest and most reckless gamble of your life is not reading the Bible, the number-one best seller of all time. Sooner or later you will see proof of life after death because you'll be a resident of either heaven or hell. Knowing this, you'd better insure your soul now with the most reliable firm, and it costs you nothing; what a deal! The firm I speak of is run by the Father, the Son. and the Holy Spirit, Inc.

**The secret of life is hope.**
**The purpose of life is to glorify God.**

Now you know. Your excuses are stripped away. Now you're on the spot. Choose. Will it be heaven or hell? If you choose hell, don't you dare blame God. It's your choice. If you choose to ignore God, when you appear before Him, you stand convicted. It's too late to change your mind and heart. Now is the time to change your mind and heart. If you ask in prayer for forgiveness of your sins, God will forgive you. Your sins, past, present, and future, were paid for on the cross when Jesus took your sins onto Himself.

God forgave King David of adultery and murder because he confessed and repented of his sin in all sincerity. But there were consequences to King David's actions. God knows we are unable to achieve perfection in this life, but we are a work in progress. Only Jesus was without sin. Jesus also said, "Go, and sin no more" (John 8:11). Today is the day to hear His knock and open your heart. Do it now and know the joy of the Lord. One day we'll all stand before God's judgment, but knowing the password, *Jesus*, we have settled out of court.

## LET'S FACE IT

A few Sundays ago I watched a TV sermon by a prominent pastor. I became so engaged that I took notes. The title was "Family Reunion." The theme was the breakdown of the family in America. These are the startling facts he presented: 50 percent of first marriages, 67 percent of second marriages, and 74 percent of third marriages end in divorce. Divorce and selfish people are soul mates. Around 50 percent of our teens are having sex, 25 percent with multiple partners. America is the number-one consumer of pornography. Around 40 percent of our children are born out of wedlock, and

61 percent of our people distance themselves from the church even though almost 80 percent claim to be Christian. The good pastor had the courage to tell it like it is; sex denied between married couples is the fertilizer for the growth of the porn industry. Any child can find a porn site on the Internet. The galleries of photos hold nothing back and are free to view; only a few videos require "proof" of age by providing a credit card number.

As if that weren't enough, another contributor that is destroying the family is illegal drugs. When I was a lad, a dope was someone who wasn't quite right in the head. Today dope is a substance taken by people who are not quite right in the head. In some countries, the drug barons have become more powerful than their governments, and with private armies of their own, they intimidate and buy off or assassinate any government official who dares to stand in their way. Drugs come across the Arizona border unchecked like a flowing river to satisfy America's addiction. The only way to stop it is for the US market to dry up. The only way to do that is for the local and federal governments to get tough with dealers and users.

Illegal drug use is not an individual choice that hurts no one; it wrecks families, and now it threatens our nation. In my state, the governor says that the second-highest budget item is the incarceration of criminals. Even so, dealers should be sentenced under federal law to thirty years without the possibility of parole. Users not only hurt themselves but their whole families and should be sentenced to at least two years of rehabilitative confinement, which would include instruction in God's Word. Too severe, you say? Remember that the idea is to stop drug trafficking in its tracks. The few prisons that emphasize a Christian education have a sharply reduced the number of returnees. We must be tougher than the drug barons by establishing a mandatory death sentence for them. I say this because they have slaughtered their opposition; the Bible is plain about this drug evil, and we the people should become God's instrument in fighting this evil.

I am at war with factions from within—the enemy with the hidden threat that has destroyed empires. America is not immune because we have run out of vaccine, the Christian education. Now a public Christian education has become the antibiotic required to save us from many of these evils and ensure us of God's blessing. There is no maybe about it.

*The solution is probably in your home. Look to your Bible for God's answer to our problems.*

Thanks again for listening. Allow me my favorite quote from history, a warning by Thomas Jefferson, our third president:

"God who gave us life gave us liberty. And can the liberties of a nation be thought secure when we have removed their only firm basis, a conviction in the minds of the people that these liberties are the gift of God? That they are not to be violated but with His wrath? I tremble for my country when I reflect that God is just; that his justice cannot sleep forever."

# RESOURCES

William J. Federer, *America's God and Country: Encyclopedia of Quotations*. (St. Louis, MO: Amerisearch, Inc., 2000).

William J. Bennett and John T.E. Cribb, *The American Patriot's Almanac: Daily Readings on America*. (Nashville, TN: Thomas Nelson, 2008).

Neil S. Wilson, ed., *The Handbook of Bible Application*. (Carol Stream, IL: Tyndale House Publishers, 2000).

Spirit Filled Bible. (NKJ version, Thomas Nelson, Inc. 1991).

www.ingramcontent.com/pod-product-compliance
Lightning Source LLC
Chambersburg PA
CBHW072014110526
44592CB00012B/1305